colour
your home

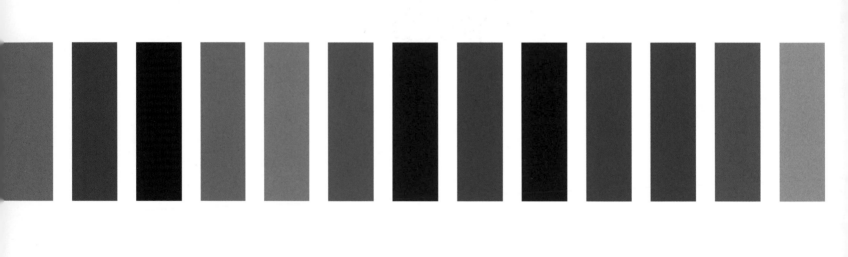

House Beautiful

colour your home
creating colour schemes that work

caroline atkins

hamlyn

First published in Great Britain in 2003 by
Hamlyn, a division of Octopus Publishing Group Ltd
2–4 Heron Quays, London E14 4JP

Text, design and layout copyright © Octopus Publishing Group Limited 2003
Photography copyright © The National Magazine Company Limited 2003
(except those listed at the back of the book)
House Beautiful is a trademark of the National Magazine Company Limited

Distributed in the United States and Canada by
Sterling Publishing Co., Inc.
387 Park Avenue South, New York, NY 10016-8810

ISBN 0 600 60602 3

A CIP catalogue record for this book is available from the British Library

Printed and bound in China

10 9 8 7 6 5 4 3 2

contents

the colour wheel

how colour works

Colour is the magic ingredient that brings rooms to life, changing the outlook and establishing the atmosphere. Each colour has its own character, so you need to get to know the colours, the settings for which they are suited, the effects they can create and the other colours they will mix with.

This book makes sense of them all. It introduces the main colour groups and suggests rooms in which they will succeed, directing you towards sources of inspiration for the exact shade you are looking for. It also demonstrates what happens to those colours when you introduce secondary shades to complement or contrast with them. In addition, it provides quick, practical ideas for adapting your existing colours with accent details, furnishing accessories and easy paint effects. First, though, you need to understand the basics of how colour works.

the magic of colour

Nothing establishes a mood as fast as colour – our reactions to different colours are instant and instinctive. The atmosphere of each room in your home will be an automatic response to the colours you use in it, so you need to be sure it is the effect you want. Depending on the colours with which you decorate, rooms can look larger or smaller, warmer or cooler, casual and relaxed or formal and dramatic. This lets you conjure up contrasting moods as distinctive as the changing seasons of the year.

▷ pastels

Pastels are the easiest, most forgiving shades with which to experiment. Gentle in tone and sweet in character, these diluted versions of stronger colours mix happily together and never fail to create a general sense of harmony. Familiar as the background for traditional nurseries and children's rooms where their soothing nature is especially welcome, pastels can also create a fresh, modern effect when combined with simple furniture styles. For a really pretty look, simply paint a few pieces of plain wooden furniture in a selection of these delicious sugared almond shades.

▷ brights

Using bolder colours requires more courage, but they will reward you richly if you choose them carefully. Use the colour wheel at the back of this book to ascertain whether the shades you are mixing will harmonize (like the blue and turquoise walls shown here) or contrast (like the blue and terracotta, or the turquoise and pink). In general, bright colours create a modern look that is more appropriate for contemporary rather than traditional furnishings. However, there is no harm in trying bright colours in a period house to establish a distinctive, vibrant style.

◁ darks

Deep colours create moody, sombre effects and a sense of real drama. You probably would not want to decorate a whole house in these shades, but their muted tones are actually more restful than the harsher brights of the group, shown below left. Match them with comfortable old leather furniture and shelves of leather-bound books, or with sleek black wrought iron and ebony for a starker, contemporary look. Earthy colours like greens and browns have a natural quality that is easy to live with, while grey and burgundy have a classic elegance of their own. Use them to add a formal air to living and dining rooms, or to conjure up a quiet, studious atmosphere reminiscent of a classic study or library.

◁ neutrals

Subtle and sophisticated, the neutral palette has a style of its own and is tremendously satisfying to use. Sometimes it is all the tone you need to accent a room's architecture, so enjoy it for its own sake, not as an absence of colour. Here, pure white, cool grey, soft vanilla floorboards and mellow coffee walls give an idea of the shades available to choose from. They create a restrained but restful combination – beautifully understated and casually chic. To decide whether you want the effect to be warm or cool, see the selection of neutrals on pages 122–125, then have fun playing with the shadows and contrasts their different tones can produce.

warm and cool colours

If you have a look at the colour wheel on page 18, you will see that different shades have different qualities of warmth and coolness. Blue is the coldest point, with blue-greens and the bluer shades of violet spreading out into a cool front on either side of it. Orange, facing it on the other side of the wheel, is the warmest point, with hot reds on one side and glowing, sunny yellows on the other. Green and violet are the crossover points, with the yellower shades of green and the redder shades of violet both becoming much warmer.

This is not just a theoretical distinction – all these colours have an instant effect on the space where you use them, letting you warm up or cool down the atmosphere to suit your mood, the function of the room and the direction it faces. For instance, north-facing rooms, which don't get much natural light, will benefit from warm colours that compensate for the lack of sunshine. Bright, south-facing rooms may need cooler colours to calm them down in the heat of the day.

△ cool

Shades of blue, aqua and lilac create a cool, fresh scheme. The emphasis is on sleek, streamlined shapes and reflective surfaces – the elegant vase, chrome lampbase and pale wood table top all have a restrained, sophisticated style that matches the cool colours.

▷ warm

Decorated in shades of red, orange and yellow, the same room takes on a rich, welcoming feel, glowing with traditional warmth. Its inviting sense of comfort is accentuated by plenty of texture – the grain of the wood and the folds of the rug on the sofa give the colours even more depth.

advancing and receding colours

As well as responding to the mood of the room and picking colours that create the right atmosphere, you need to consider whether the amount of space feels right and looks in proportion. Colour can play clever tricks here. The general rule is that light colours make a room feel bigger – these are called 'receding' colours because they give the impression of making the walls look further away than they really are – and dark shades create a cosier, smaller space – they are known as 'advancing' colours because they appear to bring the walls closer. This phenomenon is visible on a colour wheel (see page 18), where the cool shades have a receding effect and the warm shades have an advancing effect.

Put all this information together, and the result is that the darker and warmer the colour, the smaller your room will feel; the lighter and cooler the colour, the larger the room seems. White is the ultimate space-maker but pale blue comes a close second, while deep, glowing red will create the cosiest, most enclosing feel.

The three rooms pictured here show the impact of colour in altering the dimensions of the available space.

△ attic bedroom

In the attic bedroom, where the ceilings are low and the floor area more or less limited to the width of the bed, the room has been decorated in white (with a touch of lilac on the sloping ceiling) to open up the space to the maximum. This is especially important where there is not much natural light. Here, the skylight window has been left free of curtains or blinds to allow as much light as possible to flood the potentially dark corners under the eaves, and the far wall is painted bright white to reflect light back into the space. The lilac on the ceiling is a clever choice because, being one of the crossover colours where warm meets cool (see page 10), it has the space-making qualities of a receding shade but just enough warmth to take the chill off the pure white.

▽ blue bedroom

In the blue bedroom, there is a much more definite sense of colour, but the blue walls are still light enough to have a space-making effect. The deeper touches of mid-blue in the bedlinen and cushion covers, and the stronger navy and cobalt in the lampshade, flower jug and other accessories add accent and contrast to the basic colour scheme without introducing a different palette, so the total effect remains overwhelmingly blue and therefore receding. Again, the bed is fitted into a very narrow area, but because of the blue walls, and the clever use of white for the floor, furniture and curtains, the whole room feels very spacious and airy.

△ red bedroom

The red bedroom demonstrates the enclosing character of this rich shade. Although there is plenty of space between the bed and the window, the advancing effect of the red walls makes the room feel smaller and warmer, so that you feel surrounded by colour. A light-coloured floor might have pushed the walls outwards, but keeping it dark ensures that the sense of cosiness is increased. The only lighter area is the orange paintwork above the picture rail. This is still from the warm half of the colour spectrum, but because it is lighter than the red it elongates the walls to make the ceiling seem higher, and prevents the warm colour scheme from becoming oppressive or claustrophobic.

complementary contrasts

On a colour wheel (see page 18), each of the primary colours lies directly opposite the secondary colour that is created by mixing the other two primaries together. So red is opposite green (mixed from blue and yellow), blue is opposite orange (mixed from red and yellow) and yellow is opposite violet (mixed from red and blue). These opposite pairings are known as complementary colours, because of the way the two shades intensify each other. Used in combination, they are generally too dramatic a mix for comfort – don't try to use them in equal amounts or you will find they compete rather than complement each other. Instead, introduce accents of one colour to balance the other, and you will see how they both come wonderfully to life. It is a working example of the attraction of opposites.

▽ red and green

This is the strongest and most vivid of contrasts, the green making the red look even more red and the red throwing the green into sharp relief. Here, the touches of green in the sofa throw, ceramics and glassware are used to offset the predominantly red room. If it feels a bold mix to tackle, look for inspiration in natural settings where the two colours appear in combination. Think of the bright red flowers of geraniums glowing against their green foliage, or the contrasting shades in woodland as splashes of red autumn leaves start to appear among the summer greens.

▽ yellow and violet

This is a surprisingly versatile mix, able to capture the opulence of regal purple and gold, or the simple freshness of flowers in a spring garden, depending on the shades you choose and the textures in which you use them. The room shown here conveys a little of both effects, the luxurious folds of the throw adding a rich, dramatic flourish to the yellow sofa, with the pastel-coloured hyacinth blooms on the coffee table creating a softer, prettier contrast. Again, it is the balance of warm and cool that completes the effect, and again, the two colours highlight each other's character perfectly.

△ blue and orange

This is a classic combination, the cool of the blue and warmth of the orange offsetting each other perfectly. Next time you are in an art gallery or bookshop, take a look at the impressionist artist Cezanne's still-life paintings of fruit, and you will notice that the golden tones of pears and peaches are outlined by blue shadows that bring out their rich colour even more strongly. For more everyday inspiration, look at the way blue and white china works against plain earthenware ceramics and terracotta tiles in a farmhouse kitchen, or how orange-tiled rooftops stand out against a bright Mediterranean sky.

toning, harmonious and contrasting schemes

Once you understand the relationship between different

colours, you can control the effects they create when you

combine them, so that instead of relying on hit-and-miss

experiments, you are able to make confident choices.

Decorating combinations fall into three main categories of

colour scheme:

■ **toning:** where the scheme is based on varying depths of a single colour, working from a very limited palette so that the only variation is in adding lighter, whiter shades or darker, deeper tones.

■ **harmonious:** mixing shades that lie fairly close to each other on the colour wheel so that there are no jarring clashes, just gentle highlights introducing a hint of contrasting colour.

■ **contrasting:** introducing colours from opposite sides of the wheel for a stronger, more dramatic effect in which complementary shades offset each other's differences.

△ toning blues

Toning schemes are the simplest to devise, as you are essentially dealing with a single colour. However, you need to make sure you introduce enough variety within the palette so that it doesn't feel monotonous – and you need to be sure that it is a colour you can live with in quantity. Use the colour cards you find in paint-mixing shops as a guide. Each one is like an individual palette of toning colours – from the palest tints to much deeper shades. Also look at the patterns created by single colours in china, fabric and wallpaper designs. Although drawn from one basic palette, they incorporate graduated shades in different elements of the pattern. The colours in the china displayed here, for example, range from pale sky blue to much brighter cobalt and dark navy. Echoing this, the room is furnished in a selection of soft blues, including the mid-blue woodwork, the darker checks of the rug and the mixed paint layers of the bureau. There is plenty of variety here, but because all the shades come from a single segment of the colour wheel, it is a very gentle, restful scheme, with no risk of a clash.

▽ harmonious blue and turquoise

Harmonious schemes have a fresher feel, because introducing the adjacent colour on the wheel adds more interest. Here, the cool blue of the floor and the cushion has been combined with a slightly greener blue – if you move around the wheel from blue towards yellow, this is the first shade you come to – which highlights its fresh, summery look and creates a slightly Caribbean effect. There is something very satisfying about using two almost-matching colours together. The similarity keeps the whole effect unified, but the slight difference between them gives the combination an edge of excitement. For a moment you think the two colours might fight, but instead they offset each other and create an altogether richer, livelier scheme.

△ contrasting turquoise and yellow

This is a much braver mix, but contrasting colour schemes are great fun to try once you are feeling confident about colour combining. It is almost a combination of total opposites – if the blue were cooler and the yellow a warmer, orangey shade, you would have the blue-orange complementary mix explained on page 14. However, because the colours in this kitchen are used in equal quantity, pure complementaries would be an incredibly dramatic contrast and you would have a real clash. Instead, they have both been toned down so that the contrast is not quite so strong. You have still got a cool/warm contrast and the two colours are still from opposite sides of the colour wheel, but they have been picked from slightly closer positions so that they don't try to compete with one another.

▽ the colour wheel

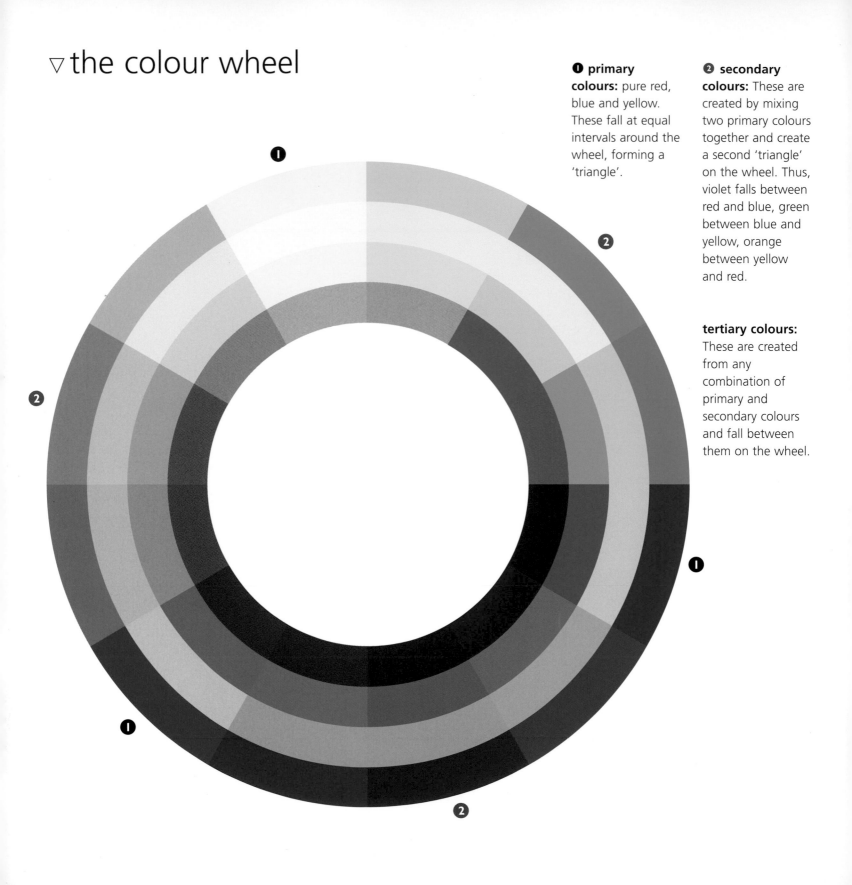

❶ primary colours: pure red, blue and yellow. These fall at equal intervals around the wheel, forming a 'triangle'.

❷ secondary colours: These are created by mixing two primary colours together and create a second 'triangle' on the wheel. Thus, violet falls between red and blue, green between blue and yellow, orange between yellow and red.

tertiary colours: These are created from any combination of primary and secondary colours and fall between them on the wheel.

the colour wheel

Most of us learn the basics of colour science when as children we memorize the colours of the rainbow – the individual shades into which white light breaks down when refracted. This is the principle on which the colour wheel is based – a complete spectrum taking you through red, orange, yellow, green, blue, indigo, violet and back to red again.

The outer circle of the colour wheel shows ❶ primary and ❷ secondary colours. You can then go on to create tertiary colours by using primaries and secondaries. The inner circles of the wheel show the subtler variations that can be created by lightening or darkening each colour to produce different tints and shades. From this layout, it is possible to see which colours will work together – harmonizing, complementing or contrasting with each other to form an effective decorating scheme.

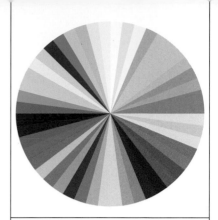

To help you plan a colour scheme, use the working colour wheel at the back of the book.

introducing colours

blue
Inspiring, spiritual, fresh, cleansing, tranquil, wise, loving, sensitive, patient, cooperative, trustworthy

purple
Idealistic, aspiring, healing, protective, regal, honourable, justice seeking, magical

pink
Romantic, mysterious, seductive, intriguing, gentle, calming, soothing, restful

red
Energetic, strong, powerful, vibrant, free-thinking, courageous, determined, independent

orange
Brave, illuminating, intellectual, confident, striving, steadfast

yellow
Joyous, invigorating, rich, opulent, intelligent, expressive, celebratory, judicious

green
Natural, rejuvenating, nurturing, optimistic, energetic, industrious, balancing, refreshing, harmonious, tranquil

mood makers
Each colour has its own natural associations, which will affect the atmosphere and mood of the room in which you use it. These qualities should be kept in mind when you are choosing decorating shades.

blue

The colour of **summer skies** and meadow flowers, blue is **fresh**, restful and inspiring. Use this failsafe decorating shade to create **tranquil** rooms with simple **elegance**.

why blue works

Blue is the classic decorating colour, taking its inspiration from a garden full of different flower shades, and finding outlets in dozens of blue and white china patterns. Fabrics, wallpapers and accessories all feel so comfortably at home in blue that it has an almost 'natural' quality – think of the robust, workaday look of denim blue, suggesting texture as well as colour.

Clean and refreshing, restful and elegant, blue is great for bedrooms and living rooms and – because of its associations with water – perfect for kitchens and bathrooms, too. Great as a background colour, easy to mix and a natural partner for plain wood, blue is endlessly variable. It can be nearly neutral in its greyer forms, verging on mauve in many of its flower shades, or bursting with exuberance in zingy Mediterranean and Caribbean palettes.

△ light reflection

Blue reflects light rather than absorbing it, so that even its deeper tones look fresh and crisp. This effect can be emphasized if you look for surfaces with their own element of sheen, such as gloss or satin-finish paintwork and areas of ceramic tiling. Similarly, lustred fabrics such as smooth silks, shiny chintz and shimmery organza all increase the effect. Rich blue or turquoise glassware on a dining table catch the candlelight beautifully, and even the glaze of blue china adds its own sparkling glow. Experiment with different blues to sample the effect of their shades. A light-reflective setting is a good opportunity to mix different blues together, as the slight translucence of the surfaces breaks up the flat colour with areas of dappled light and shadow so that the various shades blend with one another rather than clashing.

▽ tranquillity

Clear and restful, blue is a colour to wake up to and be lulled to sleep by. The paler shades, reminiscent of summer skies, are particularly tranquil for bedrooms – enhancing what 'colour psychologists' regard as the purity and healing quality of blue. Mix them with white or cream and other soft pastels for a pretty, country effect that works just as well in the town, providing a refuge of peace and quiet amid the frantic pace of modern city life. The sense of tranquillity is increased by the fact that blue is from the cool half of the colour spectrum, which makes it perfect for calming down a south-facing room that gets too much bright light. However, the result need not be cold or unwelcoming. If you want to warm up a north-facing room, opt for shades with a hint of yellow in them, such as turquoise, rather than the cooler lavender blues.

△ space enhancement

Blue is a receding colour, which means it literally seems to retreat into the distance as you look at it. This is a great advantage if you want to make a small room look bigger, as all you need to do is paint the walls blue (preferably pale blue) and they will appear to be further away. Add to this the fact that blue conjures up images of open spaces such as sea and sky, and the result is that blue can be used to create an illusion of more space. To increase the effect, stick to similar tones of blue for walls and woodwork so that you can create an impression of a more or less continuous surface rather than lots of smaller areas. Light blue is a wonderful shade for colourwashes and glazes, so you can produce that slightly translucent sense of infinite sky and limitless space.

◁ **A classic light blue is combined with contemporary, streamlined furniture and bold checks and stripes to create an elegant, timeless mix of styles.**

▷ **Curtains and blinds in warm rust-red checks and plaids stand out against the subdued blue wall to prevent the room from feeling chilly or unwelcoming.**

the blue living room

A clear sky blue gives this living room its fresh, tranquil look. This is a wonderful background colour because it lends itself to so many different styles of furnishing. There is a classic quality to it that would combine well with elegant plasterwork and deep sash windows – indeed it is very similar to the duck-egg blue traditionally used in formal drawing rooms with gilded details. On the other hand, its cool, light-reflective character also suits Scandinavian-style settings, such as the one created here. Light blue mixes beautifully with bleached wood and other pale surfaces, which add highlights that keep the whole scheme pretty and refreshing, without creating too dramatic a contrast. Here, white-painted furniture, a pale woodblock floor and cream linen chair covers provide a natural balance to the blue walls. Once you have a restful setting like this, you can vary the style of the furnishings within it. Thus the little writing table pictured here, a pretty shape designed along the traditional lines of the 18th-century Swedish Gustavian period, sits perfectly next to the more contemporary-style chairs, while the tall cabinet adds a timeless elegance.

practical accents

As well as the decorative Gustavian details and the more modern, streamlined furniture, there is a third Scandinavian-style element at play in this room. This is the more rustic, folksy angle provided by the splashes of rust red. Used in small quantities, the bold colour provides lively accents that make the room feel more lived in and cheerful, without drowning the more muted shades of the scheme. The simple checks and stripes keep the colour neatly contained, and add a practical, countrified air that is picked up in the plain woven rug on the floor. A combination of different sizes and weights of check, mixed with the occasional floral print cushion, ensures that the effect is casual and pretty rather than over-regimented.

Light reflection is important, too. The glass-fronted doors of the cabinet maximize this effect, and even tiny details such as the glass drawer handle on the desk play a part in catching the light. Keeping windows clear of fussy curtains also helps with light. Instead of being swathed with gathered fabric, this window has a neat roller blind that admits maximum light when fully raised, and is finished with floaty voile panels to provide a little privacy without obscuring the light.

texture and balance

The whole effect is neat and calm, and the blue background, offset by a balanced mixture of textures, is wonderfully cool without being cold. Modern elements, such as the aluminium filing boxes and sleek steel desk lamp, are softened by warmer, mellower accessories like the wicker footstool and traditional wooden curtain pole.

the blue bathroom

The ultimate in cool, crisp freshness, this bright bathroom really brings out the best in the blue palette. Think of a Caribbean beach – all azure sky and aquamarine water – then use those sun-drenched shades to add the same kind of holiday sparkle to a room that is feeling drab or jaded. It is a brilliant colour scheme for smallish rooms, because it lets you add plenty of colour without making the walls too oppressive. A naturally receding colour, blue – even in this relatively strong shade – creates a sense of space that is invaluable in most bathrooms. The clean quality of the colour – translucent and light reflective rather than absorbent or muted – also suits the room's simple lines and neat woodwork, with the lighter, aqua shade being used to highlight the window surround, skirting and bath panel, so that it helps define the shape of the space.

beachcombing style

Look closely at the aqua, and you will notice that it has not been applied as a flat colour, but has a slightly 'washed' surface showing different shades layered one over another. You need to be careful with this effect, because it is difficult to maintain successfully over an entire wall and, if used too liberally, can distract attention from the room's natural lines. However, it works well in small doses and specific areas like the ones shown here. It creates the impression of bleached or faded woodwork to match the seaside style of the setting and echo the other beachcomber details used to decorate the room. Shells are framed on the wall to make three-dimensional pictures in deep box frames, and the mirror is edged with coiled sailing rope decorated with ceramic starfish.

deeper accents

Even the neutral tiles around the edge of the bath continue the beach theme, picking up the slightly pink shades of the rope and shells to recreate the colour of Caribbean sand. The tiles even have a matt, unglazed finish that reinforces the effect of sand.

The deeper colours used for the towels and the window blind are simply stronger accents of the existing shades. If you look at the darker areas where natural shadows are created by the vase of flowers, the line of the window surround and the little shell pictures, you can see a deeper blue with more purple in it. This is the tone picked out by the fabrics to add a night-sky contrast to all the sunshine in the room. Lastly, a patterned trim along the edge of the blind and one of the towels combines both light and dark shades to soften the contrast so that it doesn't kill the paler colours.

four looks to create with blue

The versatility of blue means you can use it in a variety of very distinctive styles. Take a relatively limited palette of mid-blue shades, and you can coax different effects from it to create drama or simplicity, traditional elegance or modern minimalism. Blue is always responsive to new ideas, so have fun experimenting with a look to suit your setting.

△ rustic simplicity

Make use of the simple, practical nature of blue and white checks and stripes by combining gingham and plaid fabrics with traditional crockery for a clever kitchen setting. Opt for open shelves rather than flush cabinet doors and use pull-out crates and baskets for extra storage. Fix a length of painted trellis to the wall on which to hang cups and utensils, and curtain off appliances and the rubbish bin with panels of fabric.

△ gothic drama

A rich blue wall makes a great background for displaying pictures and artefacts, and creates mood and atmosphere in a dining room. Use wall lights to make the most of the glowing colour, then find strong shapes and silhouettes to set against it. Bold furniture designs and intriguing ornaments add drama and cast interesting shadows. Touches of black – for example ebony or wrought iron – look particularly effective.

28   blue

△ mediterranean mosaic

Some blues have a wonderfully translucent quality, which is perfect for bathrooms. Try mixing layers of colour – deep cobalt, bright azure and pale turquoise, for example – to create a painted mosaic pattern on a plain tiled splashback. This effect is achieved by stamping thin coats of ceramic paint in small squares, loosely positioned so as to leave occasional white highlights as contrast, with a slightly deeper shade where the colours overlap. Choose bath oils and crystals in matching colours as bathroom accessories.

△ contemporary cool

Use areas of bold paintwork instead of pictures on the walls. Blocks of plain colour like this contrast very effectively with pale wood and streamlined shapes to give a clean, contemporary look. Mix your blues with whites and creams to keep the finish cool and crisp. The effect is strong and uncompromising, but you can soften it by adding plenty of texture with layers of fabric throws and piles of comfortable cushions.

four shades of blue to try

denim

Denim blue has a muted, unobtrusive quality that blends well with greys and oatmeals. Dark but not overpowering, it is as practical as you would expect from its associations with hardwearing jeans. However, its inky tone becomes much softer when you use it in decorative fabrics or wallpapers.

- **style:** Natural, versatile, classic.
- **inspiration:** Casual fashion, sailing supply shops, monochrome fabrics.
- **where to use:** In stripes, checks and plains for kitchens, bathrooms, children's rooms and seaside settings. In elegantly patterned fabrics, papers and china for bedrooms, living rooms and dining rooms.
- **watch points:** None.
- **mix with:** Virtually anything – this is one of the most adaptable shades you can use.

1

cobalt

This uncompromising blue needs courage to use, but works well where you want to make an impact. A brilliant backdrop for displaying pictures, it defines space instantly and creates a focus of interest wherever you use it.

- **style:** Dramatic, contemporary, scene-stealing.
- **inspiration:** Mediterranean postcards, modern art.
- **where to use:** Kitchens – for an urban, high-tech look – and dining rooms. Playrooms, where it makes a great background for children's paintings.
- **watch points:** It can be very overpowering, so try out likely paint colours over a large test area to make sure you can live with it.
- **mix with:** Fresh greens, warm terracotta, sleek chrome appliances.

2

turquoise

Rich and opulent, turquoise adds instant vitality. It may be too strong for rooms that are in use all day, but it glows beautifully in early morning light, creates atmosphere for evening rooms and provides an effective accent colour when used for details and accessories.

- **style:** Vivid but therapeutic.
- **inspiration:** Caribbean seas, sari silk shops.
- **where to use:** Bedrooms and living rooms – try it for cushions and covers if you are not brave enough to paint a whole wall.
- **watch points:** Keep a check on the green/blue content of the shade – the effect can vary according to which way the balance shifts.
- **mix with:** Strong pink, most yellows (especially clean primrose and citrus shades) and contrasting orange or terracotta from the opposite side of the colour wheel.

3

sky

Intense but translucent, this is the dreamy blue of early summer. Beautifully light reflective, it creates a fresh mix with white and cream but can also take accents of stronger, contrasting blue.

- **style:** Tranquil, calming.
- **inspiration:** Summer skies, forget-me-nots.
- **where to use:** Bedrooms, bathrooms, daytime living rooms, anywhere that you want to create more space.
- **watch points:** Be careful in north-facing rooms where it could look cold.
- **mix with:** White, cream, pastels, purply-blues.

4

mixing blue with other colours

green

Don't worry about the old adage that 'blue and green should never be seen'. In fact they can make a brilliant colour combination that works in all kinds of settings – from zingy Caribbean schemes to the painted furniture of country-cottage style. Here, the balanced tones of the green paintwork and the blue wall create a strong but harmonious effect in which each colour has equal importance.

pink

Pink and blue tends to be a pretty, old-fashioned combination – especially when the shades are soft pastels like the bluebell and sweetpea colours used here. However, painting them in bold squares rather than introducing them in, for example, a floral fabric or wallpaper, creates a modern, more dramatic look, making them suitable for contemporary settings and simpler furnishings.

yellow

The traditional seaside mix of sun and sky or sand and sea, yellow and blue balance each other perfectly. Fresh and spring-like, this combination is particularly effective if you go for a bright cobalt or the turquoise-toned blue used in this bedroom, and offset it with a rich, sunny yellow. It cannot fail to cheer up a gloomy room, even in the depths of winter.

purple

Close together in tone, blue and purple can be used to create a moody, dramatic look, with the blue providing a quiet, muted background and flashes of purple adding livelier accents. Use plenty of neutrals to offset the potential colour clash, for example natural wood tones to add warmth, with slate greys and pewter-coloured metals echoing the room's more sombre undercurrent.

red

Red and blue both have a neat, no-nonsense quality that makes them the perfect mix for children's rooms and seaside schemes. As pure primary colours, they come together from different parts of the colour wheel to provide a smart contrast – not so contrary that they fight, but just enough for a robust practicality that works brilliantly well when used in checks, stripes and crisp plain cottons.

neutrals

There is no neutral shade that doesn't look good with blue, but you need to watch the effect that different shades will have. Anything with a hint of orange (the natural opposite of blue on the colour wheel), for instance, will help to intensify the blue by contrast. Greys will emphasize its cool tones, while warmer, pinkier neutrals such as the stone-coloured ceramic tiles shown here will provide a gentle balance.

sources of inspiration

Inspiration can strike in the strangest places, even when you are not looking for it. Practical household items that you see every day without really taking them in can suddenly spark an idea for a paint colour, a sofa fabric or just the shade you need to offset your bedlinen. Check your wardrobe to see how well the colours you enjoy wearing work together, and start taking note of the blues you like, wherever you come across them – anything from a pack of airmail envelopes on your writing desk to a nest of blackbird's eggs found in the garden. The vivid colours encountered during foreign holidays can be particularly inspiring, so keep an album of favourite views, postcards and souvenirs for future reference.

△ fabric departments

Ask for samples of fabric you like and start a scrapbook of favourite colour combinations so that you build up a picture of shades that work well together. Include pages from magazines showing rooms and furnishings you feel you could live with.

▷ garden blooms

Look for colours that inspire you in market stalls and flower beds. Notice how flower combinations work in natural harmony and learn to trust your instincts so that you can put colours together with confidence.

△ china and crockery

Pick shades from your own kitchen shelves or china cabinet, or take a look around a big china department for a wider selection. Blue and white is a classic mix, providing a fail-safe palette of decorating colours.

△ window shopping

Keep your eyes open for inspiration while you are on the move. It's a good idea to keep a camera with you to snap new ideas as you come across them, and then file them with your paint and fabric samples for reference.

▷ paint shops

Collect colour cards for general inspiration as well as to choose specific colours. Always try out likely shades in good-sized sample patches before making a decision, and test them against any fabrics or wallpapers you are thinking of using.

purple

Regal and opulent, subtle and **mysterious**, purple provides
unlimited atmosphere for innovative decorators. Discover the
secrets of this most **intriguing** of shades.

why purple works

This is a colour group full of extraordinary contrasts – from rich, regal purples right down to the soft, hazy shades of wisteria blossom and sugared almonds. Because it is a crossover colour on the colour spectrum, falling between blue and red and incorporating both of them in its make-up, it can be either warm or cool and – depending how you use it – can create very different looks. Paint a room in a dark shade from the red side of the colour spectrum and it will have an advancing effect, making the room feel smaller, warmer and more enclosing and filling it with drama. Paint the same room in a soft mauve from the blue side of the spectrum, and the receding effect takes over – the room is filled with cool, light space, and the atmosphere becomes soothing and restful.

△ confidence

Decorate a room in a bold purple, and you are instantly assumed to have a confident eye and dramatic approach. Yet it is the colour itself that provides the confidence. Much easier to use than most people imagine, purple manages to create a tremendous sense of drama without being overpowering or hard to live with. This is partly because a small amount will go a long way, so that you can experiment on a small scale and not feel you have to paint an entire room deep violet. Try adding details or accessories in a rich shade of heather or plum and watch the effect they have on a predominantly neutral scheme. You will notice an immediate sense of luxury and be inspired with new confidence to try bolder, more imaginative decorating ideas.

▽ romance

Nothing brings out the romance of a room quite as well as purple. It is partly the psychological associations of the colour itself – spiritual, idealistic, magical, protective – but it is also the way that purple mixes with the prettiest decorative surfaces and effects. The trick is to use iridescent or pearlized finishes that will diffuse the colour reflected in them. Sequins and crystals make perfect trimmings for cushions and lampshades, as do mother-of-pearl buttons, which already have shades of lilac and grey in their layers. Fabrics with a shimmer – from velvet and silk to translucent organza – give purple a soft silvery glow. China and glass add their own glowing colour – set a dining table with wine-coloured goblets, and pair them with lustred china (the type with a slightly pearlescent glaze) so that they catch the light.

△ subtlety

The individual shades of the purple colour card are surprisingly subtle. Colour is a notoriously difficult entity to remember, which is why it is essential that you take samples with you when shopping to match a particular fabric, paper or paint. Certainly, purple is one of the toughest to remember, slipping from one shade into another so that you can never quite put your finger on it. Almost grey in its palest forms, it merges into dark blue and deep magenta at its strongest. Because it holds so many tints of blues and reds, there is even a point where it is closer to brown than anything else.

◁ **A soft, heathery purple feels light and spacious in a busy hallway, and creates an intriguing impression as you step inside the front door.**

▷ **Soft, lemony green woodwork provides a gentle contrast against the purple background and is less harsh and more interesting than bright white.**

the purple hallway

This soft, heathery shade opens up the hallway and sets a distinctive style for its house right from the start. Stepping into an entrance like this, you know at once that it is going to be a place full of interesting details and unusual colours. The real magic is its adaptability. It is an incredibly elegant shade, restful and pretty, yet it doesn't feel too formal, so it creates the perfect background for a hallway that needs to contain all sorts of essential household items. The overall effect is relaxed and slightly bohemian, while the elegance of the colour is echoed in clever detailing and carefully chosen furniture. A decorative painted lintel is supported on carved wooden brackets, and an ornamental, slightly whimsical chandelier is matched by equally ornate wall sconces, all casting interesting shadows on to the unusual colour. The neat, painted semi-circular console table takes up little space against the wall, and a slimline hatstand holds lightweight coats and hats just inside the door.

mixed styles

This mix of the elegant and the casual extends to the woodwork, too. Instead of pure white, a soft lemony green has been used to paint the skirting, lintel and banisters, creating a more interesting, less harsh contrast with the purple walls. The unpainted surfaces add their own colour – the pale laminated floor and the darker, bamboo-style wood of the hatstand sit equally happily against the muted background, while a stack of wicker baskets provides practical storage under the stairs. It is a setting that welcomes both modern and traditional furnishings – from elegant, decorative furniture shapes to streamlined vases and contemporary-style mirrors and pictures.

light and shade

Purple is not a colour you would normally expect to find in a hall or stairway. Conventional wisdom is to choose neutral shades that can act as a link between the colours visible in other rooms, or warm sunny shades that have a positively enclosing, welcoming effect. Although this purple not a sunny shade, it is not remotely unwelcoming – there is enough red in it to take the chill off the colour while keeping it very refreshing.

There is obviously enough natural sunlight coming into this hallway. The blinds on the inner doors suggest that this is in fact a space that needs shading rather than illuminating. In a house that gets the warmth of the sun for most of the day, a shady cool hallway is a welcome retreat – the very best impression for any entrance to give.

◁ **A moody purple background establishes a dramatic atmosphere and suits the interesting mixture of modern and retro styles.**

▷ **Rich-coloured covers, dark-striped curtains and a billowing canopy complete the effect of a traveller's bedroom, full of romance and adventure.**

the purple bedroom

Layers of moody purple and violet fill this bedroom with drama and atmosphere, keeping it cool and restful but packed full of interest. In its own way, it is just as romantic as a setting complete with floral flounces and a four-poster bed, but here the romance is to do with a sense of adventure, and dreams of distant travel. The striking bed frame, piled with heavy blankets and rich silk cushions, makes a strong focal point, while the flashes of brighter colour and lighter, fluffier textures look all the more effective against the deep background.

traveller's tales

There is a hint of the exotic about purple, which makes it good for conjuring up an idea of faraway places. But this is not a spicy, over-the-top colour scheme. Instead there is something distinctly restrained and old-fashioned about it. This is partly because the mixture of deep purple with muted browns and greys creates an effect rather like a faded sepia photograph, and partly because the style of the furnishings is actually surprisingly traditional. An old-fashioned buckled chest – like a seafaring trunk but woven from seagrass and with leather hinges and fastenings – sits at the end of the bed as though waiting to be packed for the next journey. The radio beside the bed is a faithful period replica and the whole theme is complemented by a billowing length of fabric, hung

from the ceiling and swept back behind the bedhead to create a dramatic canopy reminiscent of mosquito nets and Bedouin tents. This is a traveller's retreat – the place to display ethnic artefacts and souvenirs from foreign lands, and to dream of further adventures.

interest and glamour

The moody, muted colours keep the overall effect dark and shaded, but it is never dull in this room. There is plenty of textural interest, with heavy striped curtains at the window and woven storage baskets stacked on the floor. Fringed throws and blankets knitted in chunky wools and plaids contrast with the silk cushions piled on top of the pillows – you can imagine rich-patterned kilims incorporated in this mix, too. Then there is the canopy over the bed, sheer and gauzy, and the soft rug on the floor beside it. Glamorous rather than feminine, these deep tones and rich textures have the confidence of purple but none of its occasional brashness. The curtain pole is a muted pewter colour rather than bright silver, and the bedside tables have a matt, dulled finish, like brushed aluminium. Even the combination of dark purple with rich red is completely in character – it adds a touch of excitement but is kept in check by the subtler greys and browns surrounding it.

four looks to create with purple

Sometimes dramatic, sometimes soothing, the subtle character of the purple palette can establish a surprising range of moods and styles. Use it carefully, and you will find it one of the easiest and most adaptable colours to play with. Then, once you've got more confidence, you can indulge in some of its bolder effects.

△ streamlined luxury

This is purple at its most opulent – combined with mosaic tiles, luxurious towels and a bath sunk into a deep surround-cum-seat. It is a very pure mid tone, refreshing but not cold. Flashes of bright Caribbean turquoise and soft shell pink create lively, jewel-like contrasts, while touches of silver and grey are used to maintain a practical edge amid the luxury.

△ modern romance

You cannot get much more romantic than a four-poster bed, even in a modern bedroom, and lavender-coloured linens provide a dash of pure indulgence. This is a very simple room, almost entirely white except for a few touches of natural wood and basketware, and the strong colour focuses attention on the bed's elegant lines and pretty muslin curtains.

△ bohemian chic

Combine old-fashioned florals with more modern furnishings like suede cushions and steel lamps, and you end up with a comfortable contrast with a hint of designer flair. Flowers will never go out of style – from cottagey sprigs to big cabbage roses, they appeal to traditionalists and hippies alike. This movable folding screen is a good way to try out temporary wallpaper ideas.

△ bold strokes

A muted sofa in a cool, almost-grey shade of lilac gets an injection of modernism with the strong colours and patterns of the cushions against a plain white background. The bold spotted design tempers purple into subtler, neutral colours, and the deep plum of the central cushion is picked up by the tab-top curtains. The amount of purple is minimal, but its impact is dramatic.

four shades of purple to try

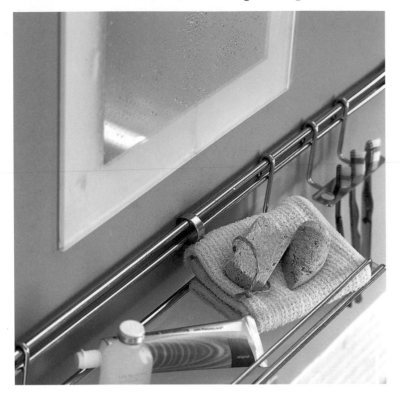

3

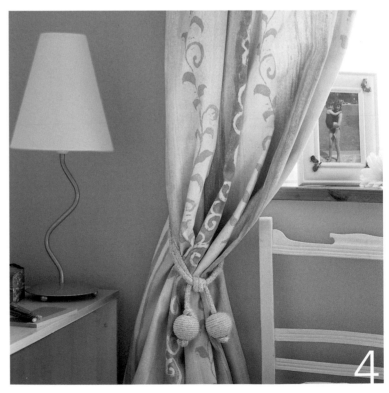

2

4

amethyst

This pure, refreshing shade is perfectly balanced between blue and pink, with a distinctive character of its own that means it cannot be mistaken for either of the others. At its best, it has a translucence like the stone after which it is named.

- **style:** Clear, jewel-like.
- **inspiration:** Coloured glass, natural crystals.
- **where to use:** Bedrooms and bathrooms, for its fresh, clean quality. As an accent colour in grey or creamy-yellow living rooms.
- **watch points:** The colour can become very intense if used over a large surface area, so make sure it doesn't overpower the room.
- **mix with:** Leaf green, clear turquoise or bright pink for contrast. Silver and pewter grey for subtler accents.

1

violet

These rich tones need courage to use, but can create a wonderful sense of luxury. The colour of teenage bedrooms and hippy style, violet is always dramatic and adds plenty of atmosphere.

- **style:** Deep, moody, dramatic.
- **inspiration:** Grapes and plums, violets and pansies, 1970s fashions.
- **where to use:** In a room that is for evening use or has good, atmospheric lighting. You need to create pools of light or it may feel too oppressive.
- **watch points:** If it feels too strong, think of the gentler shade of frosted or crystallized violets, and add silver and soft white to soften the colour.
- **mix with:** Deep burgundy for extra drama. Yellows and soft greens for natural floral accents.

2

heather

The distinctly pink tones of the upper wall here create a much warmer effect, throwing the blue into sharp relief – and also contrasting with the cushions, which are a cooler purple, more like lilac.

- **style:** Warm, pink-tinged.
- **inspiration:** Moorland walks, rockeries, wild thistles.
- **where to use:** Living rooms and bedrooms for a romantic, luxurious effect. Add silks, satins and light-reflective crystal or coloured-glass accessories.
- **watch points:** This shade needs accent and texture to break it up, otherwise it can feel a little relentless.
- **mix with:** Greens and creams for contrast. Pinks, greys and stone colours for softer accents, with old gold to add warmth.

3

lilac

The colour of summer gardens and girls' party dresses, this is an incredibly pretty shade that is easy to live with. Warmer than blue and cooler than pink, lilac is soft and adaptable.

- **style:** Hazy, cool.
- **inspiration:** Garden flowers, summer fashions, sugared almonds.
- **where to use:** Almost anywhere except dark or north-facing rooms. Restful and refreshing, it mixes comfortably with different colours and furnishing styles.
- **watch points:** Don't let it get too grey. This is a cool shade and can become gloomy in poorly lit rooms.
- **mix with:** Silver, grey and soft greens for romance. Dark chocolate brown for drama and warmth. Sugared-almond pink for pretty pastel schemes.

4

mixing purple with other colours

blue

Purple and blue are generally harmonious, so to create an impact you need to keep the two shades quite distinct, using a reddish-purple to contrast more strongly with the blue. Try the colours on two adjacent walls for a fresh, contemporary look that will work well in playrooms, kitchens and anywhere you want a lively, invigorating look.

green

The combination of soft green and hazy purple turn this bedroom into a romantic flower-garden setting. It is a restful mix – good for living rooms as well as bedrooms. Using two shades of the same strength provides a good background for adding splashes of stronger colour such as the bolder green of the checked pelmet and the jewel-bright amethyst bottle on the windowsill.

yellow

As complementary colours (see page 14), purple and yellow bring out all the strength of each other's character, so this is a chance to have fun with a really dramatic mix. Here, the predominantly purple furnishings have been livened up by painting the lower half of the wall yellow – the perfect background for a fantasy scheme of feather boas and floaty muslin drapes.

pink

Bright shades of pink and purple are fairly hot to handle, so it is best to keep them for 'outdoor' rooms or for details and accessories such as these Mediterranean-style pots. Have fun trying out different paint colours to get an idea of the various effects you can create. (For a softer, more tranquil pink and purple mix, see the pastel colour scheme on page 65.)

red

Small amounts of deep red will accentuate the mysterious, exotic character of purple, hotting up its more muted tones and creating a richer mix. Here, the striped cushion, incorporating varied shades of scarlet, burgundy and crimson, somehow wakes up the purply-greys of the bedcovers to make the whole effect far more dramatic.

neutrals

As one of the moodiest and most dramatic colours in the decorating palette, purple really benefits from quiet, neutral accents to balance its strong character. Warm shades are particularly effective, as their yellowy tones act as complementary highlights. Simply adding natural elements such as wooden furniture and storage baskets will make all the difference to a purple colour scheme.

sources of inspiration

Purple is not a colour you expect to see too often because most of its associations are either rarefied or faintly rebellious. At one end of the scale it is regal and imperial, the colour of justice and stateliness; at the other, it represents hippy hedonism and the wilder excesses of pop psychedelia. But think in floral terms, and purple takes on a much softer quality, because few other colours seem to have so many shades inspired by plants. Lilac, lavender and violet are all flowers that given their names to the purple palette, their gentler natures helping to make it a much more usable and versatile decorating colour.

△ paint samples

It is impossible to carry colour accurately in your head, so collect plenty of sample pots of paint and try them out for effect before making your choice.

◁ fresh produce

Plums, grapes, radishes, root vegetables, red onions, cabbages, aubergines and the darkest cherries all provide wonderful glossy purples to choose from. Note how good the colours look against green leaves.

△ flower petals

The deepest purples always stand out. Look for irises, hyacinths and rich dark anemones in particular.

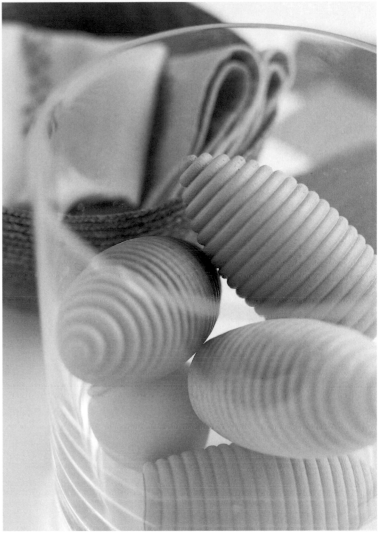

△ bathroom accessories

These are colours whose fragrance you can almost smell, so take inspiration from their pastel shades and see how pretty soaps and crystals look on a bathroom shelf.

◁ blooms and blossoms

Hazy shades like those of glorious clambering wisteria and the spreading bells of simple garden campanula capture all the subtlety of this soft, summery colour.

pink

Sugar sweet or bold and **racy**, pink is always capable of surprising you. The colour of **candyfloss**, bubblegum and **party dresses** can conjure up a host of different effects.

why pink works

Pink is the colour of calm and confidence. Even in its bolder, more dramatic shades, it is full of reassurance, and a constant source of positive energy. Warm and womb-like, the softer shades have always been a natural choice for babies' rooms, and have also been appropriated by generations of young girls as the shade that fulfils dreams of fairy-tale romance and glamour.

Pink can create an extraordinary range of decorating styles – from pretty and gentle through deep and sensuous to exotic and spicy – so don't confine it only to peaceful bedrooms. Use it in places like halls and kitchens, where its sense of vitality has a surprisingly practical effect, and try layering different shades of pink together, so that the scheme is rescued from becoming overwhelmingly sugary or too dramatic for comfort.

△ energy

Even in its paler shades, pink is naturally life-affirming, but the stronger, richer pinks have a tremendous sense of energy about them. Sometimes it is because of spicy notes that add extra warmth through their association with hot climates, but pink also has a robust, confident quality that works particularly well in contemporary settings. Mix it with industrial-style finishes such as gleaming chrome or brushed steel, and the unexpected contrast creates a stimulating effect that is good for rooms as diverse as kitchens and studies. This is intensified by the fact that strong pinks are advancing colours, giving the appearance of bringing surfaces closer towards you. A room painted or papered like this will automatically make you feel enclosed and protected – not in a claustrophobic way, but energized and able to focus your mind more clearly. Even if you are not bold enough to use it in quantity, try a strong pink in accents and details and watch the effect.

▽ romance

There isn't a colour to touch pink for glamour. Satin ballgowns, pink champagne and sexy silk underwear have all stamped it with the official seal of approval, while little girls the world over have paraded in pink party dresses and used this sweetest of shades to 'Barbie-fy' their bedrooms. Think pink, and everything suddenly seems bubbly and luxurious, encouraging you to create over-the-top effects with shimmering fabrics like silk and organza, and indulge in elaborate ruches, pleats and gathers to make the most of them. Follow through the innocent childhood image and trim your pink furnishings with festoons of ribbons and bows or hearts and flowers. Or take the more sophisticated route – pick up on the seductive theme and create the classic romantic bedroom with floaty, gauzy voiles. Drape the bed with old-fashioned satin eiderdowns in richer, sensuous shades, and add piles of silk-covered pillows and cushions to complete the look.

△ calm

Traditionally meditative and restful (its calming properties have been employed in nurseries, hospitals and even prisons to soothe the troubled mind), pink brings its own sense of tranquillity wherever you use it. The softer, coral-tinged shades are the most effective for this purpose – nothing too sharp or challenging. They look especially at home in country-style settings, where they mix beautifully with the mellow tones of old pine and natural basketware, but you can also use them very successfully in more urban colour schemes. This is not as surprising as it sounds, because warm pinks emerge quite naturally from surfaces like unrendered brickwork and plain plastered walls. Adding simple pink fabric – for curtains and blinds, for instance – continues the existing tones and helps to soften harsher elements such as dark wood and modern materials. Combine unfussy checks with plain linens and hessians to maintain the urban style.

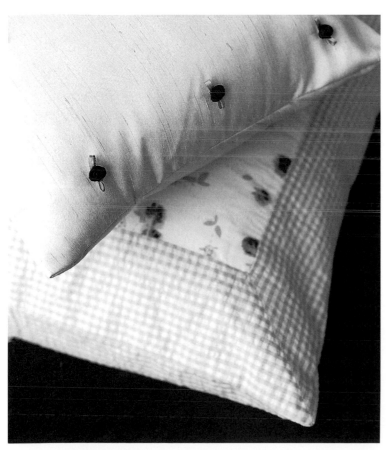

◁ **Fanciful patterns in traditional toile de Jouy fabric conjure up all the romance traditionally associated with pink bedrooms, and the elegant bed is topped with a pile of luxurious cushions and pillows.**

▷ **The delicate colour is perfect for graceful little chairs and pretty accessories.**

the pink bedroom

Soft pinks, with a warm, coral tinge, are the perfect colour for an old-fashioned bedroom furnished in traditional patterns and prints. This room manages to combine comfort with elegance. Its delicately figured fabrics and decorative shapes add a pretty, fairy-tale touch, while the plain-coloured background and inclusion of a few simpler fabrics keep the setting welcoming and lived-in rather than too perfect to touch. The starting point for the whole scheme is the classic toile de Jouy fabric used for the curtains, pillows and quilt, and the little button-back chair. Toile fabric, traditionally woven in a single colour on a white or cream background, is decorated with detailed narrative images creating miniature stories complete with cherubs, shepherdesses and entwined flowers and foliage. It comes in blue and red, among other colours – and black, for more sophisticated effects – but pink is perhaps the most fanciful, creating a bedroom that will appeal to romantics of all ages.

mixing patterns

The one thing to bear in mind with toile is that a little goes a very long way. The density of the pattern can feel very oppressive if you swathe the whole room in it, which completely undermines the purpose of using restful, soothing pink in the first place. It is therefore important to break it up with stretches of plain colour and a few more muted patterns. Bedrooms provide plenty of opportunity to mix your fabrics, because you can layer contrasting covers on the bed, and pile it high with pillows and cushions in different colours. Here, the quilted toile cover is offset by a lining in simpler pink and white striped ticking and by crisp white linen sheets. Creating a similar effect at the window, the full-length toile curtains are paired with a neat London blind with ticking on its inner side, so that just a small border of toile appears along the lower edge to contrast with the stripes. The walls are plain and the floorboards are painted pure white to provide a slightly rustic background for all the pretty patterns. A simple woollen rug adds a dash of stronger pink to draw out the room's deeper tones.

decorative details

There is something about this very pretty pink, as well as the room's elaborate fabric patterns, that makes it a natural partner for decorative furniture shapes. Look for elegantly crafted wrought iron, which will add graceful lines even if the iron itself is dark. Try painted, carved wooden furniture, such as the little bedside table, and finish the room with romantic, ornamental details such as chandeliers and lampshades hung with crystal droplets.

the pink kitchen

Strong touches of bold pink are all that are needed to add colour to this predominantly white kitchen. Sleek and modern, it relies mostly on reflective surfaces and textural contrast for its interest. The room has an industrial, high-tech feel, so that the flashes of pink provide a more lighthearted element, breaking up the cool, efficient run of streamlined units with moments of fun. Because this pink is of the strong, energetic variety, it emphasizes the room as a functional setting, rather than calming it down in the way a softer shade might. It is just enough to balance the chrome appliances, but still knows its place as part of a practical workstation. It is a confident statement to make, but not a difficult look to devise, as it lets you add decoration gradually, with the plain white background always there as a safe harbour to retreat to whenever you have doubts about using strong colour. Painted in occasional panels, the pink is much less intimidating than an entire wall, but provides a dramatic background or frame for fittings such as clocks and mirrors.

bold contrasts

The pink/silver contrast is an interesting one, because in a less utilitarian setting it would be expected to create a distinctly girly, romantic effect. Think of shell pink with silver trimmings, party dresses with sequin decoration, nail varnish and glitter make-up. By using the pink here in such small quantities, and restricting the silver

decoration to regimented blocks on the cupboard doors – with just an echo in the tiling along the back of the worktop – this room creates a quite different effect. Cool, calm and collected, it provides a restrained background, leaving the appliances uncluttered and ready to work. Neat chrome handles and a plain woodblock floor maintain the functional approach, and contribute to an almost 1950s feel, in which the appliances themselves are the stars and the touches of pink help to glamorize them.

modern metallics

To make even more impact, the bold pink has actually taken over the practical role in a few key places. Rather than just provide a pretty contrast, it has transformed some of the metalware into lively, colourful kitchen utensils with their own distinctive character. These metallic pinks catch the light with a rosy glow, reflecting their colour on to the white cupboards and opening up the opportunity for prettier touches where you want to add them. Storage containers, drinking beakers, even a simple colander, all in gleaming pink, create a sleek display in perfect keeping with that 1950s utilitarian chic.

four looks to create with pink

From deep rose to palest almond blossom, pink offers a wide and varied palette and a mass of different effects. The same shade can go modern or traditional, conjure up dramatic energy or blissful romance. It's all a question of where you use it and the furnishings with which you combine it, so choose your look carefully.

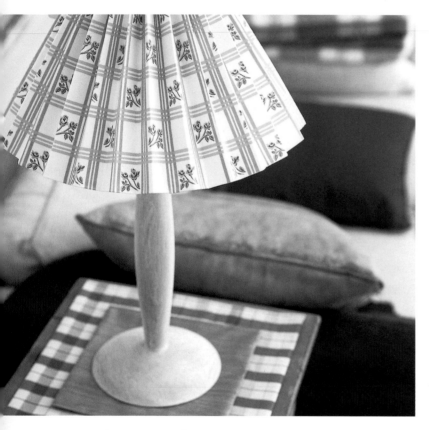

△ country casual

Pick up on the garden theme suggested by floral pinks and mix them with touches of mossy green for a fresh, country-style effect. Avoid fabrics or wallpapers with large, obvious flowers and opt instead for neat sprigs that are easy to combine with casual checks. Start by including a gingham lampshade or a few sofa cushions, then add a plaid throw to introduce more pattern and different weights of check.

△ modern paintwork

Bold blocks of colour and simple painted furniture give a clean, contemporary look with a distinctive edge. Floors can be painted using specialist, hardwearing floor paint. Alternatively, to get the exact shade that you want, use emulsion, then a few coats of clear matt emulsion to protect the surface. Look out for blank medium-density fibreboard (MDF) furniture designs that come ready to paint.

△ old-fashioned charm

Pink is the natural colour for floral fabrics, so indulge yourself with big, splashy rose and peony patterns, and let them dictate a more romantic, fanciful style of furnishing. Decorative woodwork and soft paint colours are the perfect match for these fabrics. Use gathers and ruffles to reflect their pretty, feminine look and add old-fashioned ornamentation with gilt highlights, delicate china and sparkling crystal droplets.

△ traditional panelling

For a muted, sophisticated pink colour scheme, choose a dusky shade and use it as a background colour. This deep pink has an earthy quality, similar to traditional terracotta with a dash of rose mixed in, making it wonderfully warm and restful. It is the perfect colour to use on painted wood panelling, which adds more depth by providing interesting shadows and accents.

four shades of pink to try

shell

The softest and subtlest of pinks, this is a pure classic. It is the traditional colour of fairy-tale romance, but it never goes out of fashion so you can use it to create simpler, more modern effects, too.

- **style:** Pretty, pastel, delicate.
- **inspiration:** Sugared almonds, fondant icing, marshmallows, cherry blossom.
- **where to use:** Bedrooms and bathrooms, where its restful, soothing qualities comes into its own. Living rooms – it is a warm enough shade to provide a cocooning effect and take the chill off gloomy rooms.
- **watch points:** Avoid strong colour mixes – it is too delicate to cope with them and will just look sickly in the background by comparison.
- **mix with:** Whites, creams, very soft pastels (stick to sugared almond shades).

1

candyfloss

If you want to go thoroughly over the top without quite leaving your childhood behind, this could be the pink to go for – a strong shade that can hold its own against nursery-style primary colours.

- **style:** Sweet, intense, unsophisticated.
- **inspiration:** Bubblegum, sherbet, strawberry milkshake.
- **where to use:** Children's rooms, kitsch bedrooms, retro-style kitchens (think 1950s American milk bar).
- **watch points:** This is an uncompromising shade and you need to be sure you can live with it. It is great fun, but you may not want fun on a full-time basis.
- **mix with:** Strong pastels and fresh complementary greens, such as grass or lime.

2

fuchsia

This dramatic pink creates an instant impact – good for adding an exotic touch or for revitalizing a room that needs a bit of a shake-up. Bright and contemporary, it is fun to use in practical settings where you would not expect it.

- **style:** Zingy, modern, hot.
- **inspiration:** Turkish delight, sari silks, teenage fashions.
- **where to use:** Modern kitchens – with sleek silver or chrome accessories. Dramatic bedrooms – to recreate an Eastern palace.
- **watch points:** It can be harsh and uncomfortable for an entire room, so if you are nervous about using it, try it as an accent colour or blend it with adjacent hot colours on the colour wheel.
- **mix with:** Fiery oranges and warm reds to give it more depth. Cool greens and zingy, sherbetty yellows for contrast.

3

old rose

Strong but subtle, this deep shade has a distinctive character incorporating tinges of brown and red. It is good for creating old-fashioned effects, as it gives the impression of having faded from a stronger colour.

- **style:** Faded, traditional, classic.
- **inspiration:** Faded velvet curtains, raw plaster, dusty terracotta, old brickwork.
- **where to use:** Bedrooms, dining rooms, living rooms – places where you want to create warmth and atmosphere.
- **watch points:** Be careful in rooms that don't get much light – although it is warm, the deep tone can become gloomy in darker corners.
- **mix with:** White, creams and pinky neutrals. Mossy greens and faded golds.

4

mixing pink with other colours

blue

Pinks and blues make interesting contrasts, and the bolder shades can be surprisingly dramatic. Take inspiration from the exotic colours of sari silks and try combining rich turquoise with hot fuchsia. You would have to be very brave to base an entire scheme on this mix, but it creates wonderful accents for cushions, curtains and other accessories.

green

A classic country combination, pink and green bring a sense of the garden indoors. If you are not sure where to start, look for floral pinks and then picture the leaf colours that offset them naturally in the garden. It is hard to go wrong with this mix, but novice decorators will probably feel happier sticking to soft, manageable shades rather than trying to play with more adventurous lime green and fuchsia.

yellow

Pink and yellow is not one of the first decorating combinations to spring to mind, but this is a fresh, summery mixture, reminiscent of sweetshop counters and floral dresses. It is almost a clash, but because the two tones are of equal strength and density, neither colour dominates the scheme.

purple

Keep the tones soft, and purples and pinks will be natural partners – close in shade and easy to use. This pretty tiled floor, alternating the two colours with white, is perfect for a tranquil bathroom, especially when combined with warm woods, which add a practical, contemporary touch and prevent the scheme from becoming sickly or sugar-sweet.

red

If you are going to mix red and pink, you need to go the whole hog and pick shades that look as though they are enjoying the confrontation. Here, the deep raspberry walls get reflected light from the white ceiling. This keeps them fresh and glowing so that the touches of stronger poppy red don't overwhelm them. Instead, the red curtains and flowered bedcover add extra richness and romance.

neutrals

Delicate pinks are easy to drown – even with neutral colours – so be careful how you treat them. You may find that pink-tinged stone and coffee shades work better than yellower, biscuity beiges. This room combines the two in a perfectly balanced mix, so that the washed-out neutrals of the upholstery stay muted in comparison with the pink blooms of the floral fabric.

sources of inspiration

You would expect pink to be a rare commodity – something of a luxury indulgence rather than an everyday colour. But it turns up surprisingly often, so you won't be short of decorating inspiration. Gardens full of flowers and blossom are the most obvious place to look, but you will also come across a host of pinks in your bathroom and bedroom – from lipsticks and nail varnishes to all those containers of pretty pastel products lined up along the edge of the bath. Best of all, pink is one of the most appetizing of colours, so you will find familiar shades in all sorts of edible forms from ice creams and sorbets to milkshakes and candyfloss.

▽ dress sense

Pick out colours you like from among your clothes and accessories. For an unconventional palette like pink, it helps to build your confidence by trusting shades you already know you can live with.

△ summer fruits

Fresh colours such as crushed raspberry look as good as they taste. The deep pink of the fruit can be diluted by sugar syrup, softened by a swirl of cream or ice cream, or sharpened by a sprinkling of caster sugar to give a range of different effects.

△ rose gardens

Cut flowers and garden blooms present dozens of shades for you to choose from. The softly furled petals of old roses are full of varied tones that change subtly as the heads open and then start to fade.

△ ice cream parlours

Look for pastel pinks that sit perfectly alongside creams, whites and other soft shades. These soft textures will emphasize the gentle quality of the palest, prettiest pinks.

▷ sugar frosting

Take inspiration from the memory of childhood teas and decorated birthday cakes. Bright sugar icing, coloured by a few drops of cochineal, is an unmistakably nostalgic shade.

red

If you could measure the **temperature** of colour, red would
top the list. Use it to bring **warmth** and **drama** to empty or
cold rooms and **confidence** to homes that feel tame or timid.

why red works

Strong and vibrant, red is not for the fainthearted. If you can find the courage to use it, you will discover a wonderful range of colours that bring rooms instantly to life with drama and warmth. Psychologically, red is a force for freedom and determination, so it is a great colour to use where you want to create a sense of energy or positive thinking.

Deep reds make a wonderful backdrop for dramatic dining rooms and book-lined studies. Bright berry is fresher and easy to live with – good for practical touches in kitchens and living areas, while the hotter, racier reds will warm up gloomy rooms with a hint of adventure. Think of rich terracotta and deep crimson – or even a mix of the two – for an exotic touch reflecting the spice shades of North Africa and the silks of India and the East.

△ luxury

Combined with sensuous textures and other rich colours, red becomes wonderfully luxurious, the colour of grand drawing rooms and Eastern palaces. The sumptuous softness of velvet, the warmth of fur or suede and the gleam of silks and satins all respond well to this most opulent of shades. It is a colour you want to sink into with a supply of champagne and your favourite chocolates. You don't need much of it to conjure up the right effect, so if you are more used to decorating with pastels or neutrals, take it slowly. Use warm creams and taupes to set the scene quietly, graduate to richer shades such as golds and yellows when you feel more confident, and hot things up with splashes of luxurious red.

▽ warmth

The most advancing of all colours, red is perfect for making rooms feel cosy and warm. A rich colour like this will surround you in comfort, enclosing the space to make it feel safe and protected. It will also react wonderfully with soft textures, which give the colour more depth so that it doesn't appear as a flat surface. Look for blankets and throws that can be layered for the warmest effect, and try fabrics such as felt and brushed cotton, which have a dense, absorbent finish that retain light and heat. Self-patterned jacquards, which have lots of texture in the design of their weave, are just right for squashy red sofas and armchairs, providing an inviting space in which to curl up in comfort.

△ drama

It is no good trying to be understated with red – this colour was never meant to hide its light under a bushel. So make the most of its extrovert personality and use it to create a room full of drama and excitement. A perfectly ordinary room painted in red will take on a whole new character – confident, energetic and bold. Good lighting – which means plenty of candles on special occasions – will make the walls glow and create interesting shadows, while adding over-the-top materials such as crystal and gold will make the whole scene doubly dramatic. Mirrors and gleaming metallics are important for sparkle and reflection, so look for gilded photo and mirror frames to achieve this, and choose furniture in dark polished wood furniture that will catch the light.

◁ **Deep red walls and upholstery are bold and dramatic in contrast with the pure white floor and paintwork of this contemporary-style sitting room.**

▷ **Soft velvety roses bring out the gentler, more romantic character of the red palette, combined with simple gingham checks for a country-style setting.**

the red living room

This is a room of extraordinary contrasts – a warm, classic red creating a cool, contemporary setting. The furnishings are simple, yet the effect is invitingly comfortable because of the colour used, a clear shade with a purity of tone that turns out to be surprisingly versatile. What makes the room work is its simplicity. The streamlined shape of the furniture and the straight-up-and-down lines of the fireplace are perfectly suited to the dramatic colour scheme which, for all its richness, is very clean. There is just the one red, used for the walls, the sofa and the little upholstered footstool, contrasting with the white of the woodwork – a crisp, bright white on the painted floorboards and a slightly creamier shade on the fireplace and skirting.

balance and accent

Overall, it is a beautifully proportioned scheme. Comprising roughly two-thirds red to one-third white, the colour scheme doesn't suffer from the clash that you can end up with if you use two contrasting colours in equal quantity. The red definitely has the upper hand, but the touches of white offset it perfectly. Red and white can be a tricky combination – the strong contrast is sometimes too stark and harsh for comfort – but there is a light, fresh touch at play here that prevents it falling into that trap. The red has a gentle, pink tinge to it, which you can see along the back of the sofa where the light

falls on it, and this creates a softer, textured effect. It is a bit like the texture of the velvety roses on the mantelpiece – another touch that saves the room from harsh overkill. The only accent colours are the dark green of the foliage, the natural complementary shade to red (see page 14), and the broad orange stripe across the cushion, which actually manages to make the red look sedately restrained by being even hotter and spicier itself.

focal points

In a room where the main features are so large and dominant, smaller details and accessories are important in providing a sense of balance, breaking up the expanse of colour and creating other focal points to interest the eye. Here it is achieved by a pattern of repeated images – the column-like stripes on either side of the fireplace, the silver stars along the top, the little jugs of roses on the mantelpiece and the rows of reverse-coloured dots across the cushion. There is sparkle, too, in the way the light catches the glass jugs, the glowing berries in the arrangement behind the sofa, and even the steel joints of the sleek little angled lamp.

◁ Colourwashed panelling provides a
flame-red contrast against the yellow
painted skirting board and more sombre
pewter shade of the floorboards.

▷ Glowing terracotta walls enliven this
small stairway and landing, filling the flat
with colour and creating a dramatic
entrance for a brave decorative scheme.

the red staircase

This is an incredibly brave decorating scheme for such a confined
space – especially for what is in effect the entrance hall to an
upstairs flat. The reason it works is partly because it is carried out
with such confidence and obvious enjoyment, and partly because
it gives the hallway such a strong character. Halls and landings are
often treated as nothing more than a transit area, without much
imagination being spent on them, but the strong colour scheme
and inventive details turn this one into a room in its own right, not
just a corridor leading to somewhere more interesting. Most
intriguing of all, using a hot, advancing colour doesn't seem to have
reduced the space or made it feel claustrophobic. Instead, the warm
orangey-red manages to open up the space, leading the eye up the
stairs to the little living room that has been created on the landing
above. Because there are so many details and accent colours to
interest you in the distance, you are barely aware of the limited
space on the stairs.

intricate patterns

The overall impression is spicy, exotic and vaguely Moroccan. The
flaming colour of the walls is highlighted by a deeper red in the
woven kilim and by streaks of purple and turquoise – a delicious
clash so vivid you can almost smell it. Against these colours is set
the muted purply-brown wood of the floorboards, the chunky,
low-level table and the dramatic carved masks on the wall. The
scene is enlivened by bold paintwork patterns reminiscent of North
African tiles and architectural design. The window is edged with a
border of elegant minaret-shaped motifs, a jagged pattern like
inverted bunting runs up either side of the stairs, and the stair risers
themselves are painted in extraordinary detail so that each one
looks like a row of authentic ceramic tiles.

playing with light

For a small space with a huge amount of colour crammed into it,
the staircase and landing has to use clever tricks to make the most
of the available light. If you look closely at the walls you will see
they have a patchy, textured finish, a little like rough plaster, with
different tones painted over one another to create a colourwashed
effect. Breaking up the flat colour like this makes it more reflective,
so that instead of absorbing light it bounces it back into the space
and makes the whole area glow. Panels of hand-painted colour
around the edge of the window play games with the light, too,
creating an impromptu stained-glass effect. Additional light
patterns are supplied by punched-metal lamps and a string
of fairy lights entwined around a cluster of twisted branches.

four looks to create with red

Deep red can be bold and contemporary or rich and classic. The style you create depends on the furniture, the fabrics, the accessories and the way you put them together. Always dramatic and often uncompromising, red is a strong character to deal with, so look for furnishings that can hold their own against its dominant nature.

△ baroque splendour

Indulge in the luxury of a deep roll-top bath and a setting of real old-fashioned drama. The bath itself is decorated with a band of painted fleur-de-lys motifs and looks even more imposing because of the raised plinth on which it stands. Pictures and mirrors add more opulence against the ruby-red walls, and the black and white tiled floor creates a bold contrast.

△ creature comforts

Exploit the warming, enclosing tones of rich red upholstery by piling chairs and sofas with plenty of fluffy, furry texture. Thick woollen blankets and knitted cushions, soft sheepskins, Angora rugs and heavily fringed throws all increase the sense of luxury, so layer the contrasting fabrics together for maximum impact, then sit back and enjoy the comfort.

△ classic elegance

Glowing red walls provide a glorious background for traditional-style paintings and gilded frames, and reflect the firelight beautifully. Old leather-bound books and polished brass accessories create the look of a library or study. The crackle-glazed finish of the painted fireplace surround contributes to the aged, classical look of the room.

△ country checks

This is a modern version of a traditional country look, with painted furniture and large checks adding a colourful touch to the natural wickerwork and coir flooring. Red makes a neat, fresh impression against the gentle cream background, and is picked out in smaller details such as the patterning of the toile de Jouy bolster and the gingham ribbon trim.

four shades of red to try

1

2

3

4

berry

This startlingly fresh red is an energy booster with a pretty tinge to it. Deep but clean, it can be used to create dramatic contrasts in both modern and traditional settings.

- **style:** Crisp, glowing, energetic.
- **inspiration:** Fresh cherries, winter berries.
- **where to use:** More places than you would think. This shade is pure and light reflective so although it is very strong, it has a translucence that doesn't dominate too much.
- **watch points:** Don't worry too much – if you are set on red, this is one of the easiest to try.
- **mix with:** Dark woods for a rich, traditional effect. White paintwork and crisp cottons for a simple country look.

1

terracotta

One of the most natural reds, this exudes a sense of comfort and welcome instead of trying to create a impact. It has a mellow, autumnal feel and is easier to live with than the more dramatic shades.

- **style:** Warm, inviting, comfortable.
- **inspiration:** Farmhouse floors, garden flowerpots.
- **where to use:** Living rooms and dining rooms, where you want guests to feel welcomed and enclosed. Mediterranean-style kitchens with chunky, Provencal-style earthenware.
- **watch points:** Be guided by the naturally brown tones of the shade and don't try to force pink-tinged reds into the scheme – they won't look comfortable.
- **mix with:** Harvest golds and russets to enrich the look. For contrast, fresh greens such as emerald and grass, and deep sapphire and turquoise blue. Flower colours that look good against their terracotta pots.

2

scarlet

Traditionally outrageous and rebellious, scarlet has its positive side in decorating terms. Think of it as the colour of confidence and determination and use it to create an impact.

- **style:** Hot, dramatic.
- **inspiration:** Wild poppies, London buses.
- **where to use:** Studies and kitchens, to provide energy and stimulation when there is work to do.
- **watch points:** It is very hot, so possibly not so suitable for bathrooms, where you want to keep a refreshing feel.
- **mix with:** Blues and yellows for a children's room decorated in primary colours. Black or pewter-finish wrought iron for a more dramatic look.

3

old burgundy

Naturally mellow, this is a colour that doesn't want to fight. It is perfect for restful settings and faded furnishings rather than anything too sleek and modern.

- **style:** Mellow, faded, dusty.
- **inspiration:** Old roses, sun-bleached paintwork.
- **where to use:** Living rooms that catch the late-afternoon sun. Studies with comfortable chairs and old books. Cushions, covers and curtains in soft velvet and subtly patterned damask.
- **watch points:** It has a soft, earthy quality, so don't jar it with bright colours – keep the accents harmonious.
- **mix with:** Antique cream paintwork, dark wood and dark leather furniture. Accents of old gold and rubbed gilt.

4

mixing red with other colours

blue

A bold red needs colours that can stand up to it, so look for an equally strong blue that will makes its own mark. The blue accessories used here shift from bright cornflower to a more purply bluebell shade, creating a distinctive palette that contrasts with the red and isn't overwhelmed by it.

green

Green is the natural complementary colour to red (see page 14), so this is bound to be a lively mix. The two colours bring out each other's strengths but can be a bit much to take in combination, so use them carefully. Set them side by side and the colours can zing like neon, so an entire room in red and green would be hard work. Instead, try adding green details to accent a red room, or combine red and green accessories in a neutral setting.

yellow

Two warm colours together make this a rich, opulent combination, good for adding instant warmth and creating lively, welcoming settings. Try to balance the richer golds with paler lemon and primrose shades. Here, pale chiffon curtains at the window make the most of the sunlight and there are plenty of fresh yellow flowers to prevent the colours from looking *too* hot.

pink

A red and pink mix is always going to be over the top, so play these energetic shades at their own game and add touches of gold to complete the effect. Pictures, candle holders and gold leaf or gilt paintwork will all do the trick. Pick out the different tones and use them where they feel most comfortable – the softer pink for light-filtering muslin curtains for example, and the brighter red for a vase of vivid flowers.

purple

Unless you want a really strong, dramatic effect, reds and purples are best mixed in different shades and layered tones rather than solid blocks of colour. This way, you can bring out the pinkier accents of the red, and the softer, floral notes in purple, to create a gentle combination.

neutral

For a really dramatic effect, consider adding red to neutral rather than the other way round, and use accents of red to bring a minimal cream or white room to life. A single splash of red can look slightly gory, so try mixing a few shades of scarlet and orange to create a flame-like effect with more warmth to them.

sources of inspiration

You don't have far to look for inspiration, because the red palette is full of natural colours that have given their names to individual shades. Tomato, cherry, poppy and berry are all old favourites, as well as those deep, plummy reds more familiar from the wine cellar. The traditional colour of traffic lights and London buses, red also conjures up the country shades of harvest and autumn, and the dusty terracotta of Mediterranean countries. Think of red-tiled roofs against summer skies and bright geraniums on whitewashed windowsills. For mellower shades, there are old roses and faded velvet curtains, leather volumes on the shelves of book-lined studies and the sun-bleached clay of garden pots.

△ wine cabinet

Glorious wine colours from burgundy and claret to sherry and port provide a rich palette of classic reds for you to choose from. The deeper, darker tones are almost purple, while some lighter wines suggest fresher, pinker shades.

◁ flower shops

See how florists combine toning reds in a single bouquet – velvety rose shades, crimson anemones and scarlet tulips all offsetting one another and creating deep layers of rich colour.

△ sweet counters

Sweet shops are full of primary colours, and red is a perennial favourite – the colour of aniseed twists and sugar candies among many others.

△ fruit and berries

The fresh colours of summer fruits are deliciously usable – take inspiration from raspberries, strawberries, cherries and redcurrants and make the most of their glossy, glowing surfaces.

◁ salad days

Crisp market garden shades include deep crimson radishes and pinky-red lettuce leaves, as well as the bright orangey red of tomatoes and peppers.

yellow

Let the **glow** of yellow into your home and watch it transform everything it touches. **Yellow** has powerful associations with **gold** and **sunshine** as well as simpler pleasures.

why yellow works

Yellow never fails to surprise. Warm and glowing, the colour of sunshine will lighten the gloomiest corners and fill your home with optimism. Yet it can also have a subtler, fresher quality that is restful rather than stimulating. The richer tones create an effect of classical elegance, perfect for mixing with gilded accessories, while the softer, more delicate shades suit contemporary settings and simpler furnishings.

Unexpectedly mellow, yellows are also easy to blend and mix, so that bright gold, sharp lemon and pale primrose will work together rather than clashing, letting you create schemes with great depth and richness from this single colour palette. At its subtlest, where it is almost indistinguishable from cream, yellow can be used as a very effective neutral to offset both purer whites and stronger colours.

△ richness

This glowing colour makes a brilliant background for furnishings and display items, both modern and traditional. Gilt-framed paintings will look dramatic and opulent, while cooler metals and modern fittings will stand out in smart simplicity. A strong shade, but still relatively pale against the rest of the colour spectrum, yellow is wonderfully light reflective – an excellent colour to use in basement, ground-floor or north-facing rooms. Where other, cooler reflecting colours will bounce the light off their surface, yellow attracts it almost like a magnet, absorbing it so that it seems to emit its own natural sunshine. Rich yellows are exciting to use, bold and stimulating in their effects. Think of them in terms of exotic spices like cinnamon and saffron, or imagine the warmth of sweet, buttery caramels, and let them enrich your furnishings.

▽ harmony

If the thought of yellow is too bold for you, look for the softer shades that make less impact but have their own quiet elegance. There is nothing brash or over-confident about these colours: pale primrose and lemon sorbet, for example, are restful and soothing shades. They are perfect for living rooms and bedrooms and for creating sophisticated settings when combined with pretty, graceful furnishings. Try mixing them with creams and soft whites, so that they blend into a much cooler, less stimulating shade. The closeness of these colours will melt them into what looks like a single overall background colour, against which you can add splashes of bolder accents if you want to – pinks and oranges to spice things up, or blues and greens to maintain the cool serenity. In this type of setting, even touches of bright gold will look elegant rather than brassy.

△ freshness

Natural flower shades always look fresh and pretty, and the yellow of spring flowers, the first colour seen in the garden after the barren winter months, is particularly good at conjuring up a sense of newness and rejuvenation in the home. Yellow is a natural partner for floral patterns and mixes well with all kinds of greenery, whether entwined together in fabric or wallpaper designs, or arranged as flowers and foliage in a fresh display. Clean and spring-like, yellow has an informal neatness that suits practical kitchen settings – again, try yellow fabrics in stripes and checks to create a country-style effect. It is also wonderfully bright and welcoming for hallways – nothing gives such a lively first impression as a hall painted in cheerful sunshine yellow.

the yellow bathroom

Yellow might not be the first colour you think of for a bathroom because it doesn't have the natural watery associations of blue and green, or the cool purity of white. However, this is a bathroom where you will want to linger, relaxing in the warm glow of the walls. There is no hint of chill here – you could never accuse a yellow bathroom of being cold or unwelcoming, so you instantly avoid any risk of the room feeling clinical.

shade and texture

Apart from the multi-coloured floor and the deep-blue exterior of the bath, the yellow is pretty unrelenting here, but because it is broken up by different surfaces, and because there is plenty of variation in the shades used, it doesn't become overwhelming. Walls, ceiling, woodwork and tiles all contribute a different yellow to the mix, and the tiles add texture. The glaze on the tiles is predominantly glowing and light reflective, but the slightly dimpled surface has a mottled, shadowy effect that creates brighter highlights and patches of deeper tone.

The mosaic floor is created from hundreds of tiny, rich-coloured tiles to provide an appropriately optical effect. From a distance, it appears as a strong, boldly patterned contrast to the other plain colours elsewhere in the room. As you get closer, however, you can see that it is largely composed of shades of mellow yellow and gold,

with a scattering of deep blue to add drama. Yellow, ochre, apricot, terracotta and russet are all natural earthy shades that work in harmony together and blend comfortably from one into another, while the blue accents – the blue of a Mediterranean sky – create a perfect link between floor and bath.

design details

The bath itself, freestanding and claw-footed, adds its own sense of luxury. A generous shape like this, with its deep tub and roll-top edges, turns bathing into a real pleasure. It also makes the room feel more 'furnished' and less like a collection of fittings. Seeing the bath as a piece of furniture and choosing it for its elegance and proportions as well as for its function, gives you a different eye on the room as a whole and wakens the imagination to other interesting design ideas. Pictures and mirrors on the walls help to make it feel lived-in, and their luxurious gilded frames look splendid against the glowing walls. The claw feet of the bath add a beautiful cast-iron detail against the mosaic floor and are painted gold for a final touch of opulence.

◁ **This little tub chair with its pile of contrasting cushions shows the subtle variety of golds, creams and yellows available within this cheerful palette.**

▷ **A rich, welcoming living room scheme full of mellow warmth is accented by touches of metallic gold, textured fabrics and pale yellow stone.**

the yellow living room

This living room is a brilliant example of how well different shades of yellow and gold can be mixed together. From pale primrose, through old gold and rich sunflower to bright orange, there is barely a yellow that is not represented here. Yet they all blend happily and with great versatility, providing contrast, variety and a wonderful sense of welcome in an irresistibly comfortable setting. Because the various yellows manage to create between them a background in a more or less unified tone – one of mid-depth with plenty of warmth – the room can afford to be busy and heavily accessorized without feeling cluttered. Even the natural materials in the room contribute to the effect. The woven baskets, wicker chair and rich-grained coffee table all pick up the deeper golden tones, and even the sandstone fireplace, although a far more muted, cooler shade, contains its own accents of yellow.

elegant lines

Best of all, yellow is timeless. Some colours seem to belong to a particular age, so that it can be hard to adapt them to new uses. This is not the case with yellow. Take away the furniture, and this shade could be the backdrop to a room of any period because it has a classical richness as well as a modern vitality. Yellow also translates with equal confidence and subtlety into traditional and contemporary furnishing styles. Whether casual and layered or

sleek and streamlined, its pale but uplifting tones have a natural elegance that is easy to live with. Here, that elegance is echoed by the classical lines of the fireplace, the pretty French doors with their graceful, gently arched windows, and the decorative shapes created by the gilded letters displayed against the wall.

neutral accents

What gives the colour scheme extra depth, though, is the amazing variety of texture. Thick knitted blankets and plaids, sheer organza curtains, silks and embroidery, woven basketware, the smooth gleam of metal and the matt surfaces of terracotta and stone all add tone and texture to enrich the whole picture. The carpet provides a velvety background, while the chunky alcove shelves create deep shadows which are highlighted by the broad streaks of paler paintwork across their front edge. It seems incredible that so much interest can be coaxed from a single colour, but it is made possible by the versatility of the yellow palette, and by the judicious use of neutral shades to provide just enough subtle contrast without breaking up the scheme. The pale carpet, for example, chosen to match the stone of the fireplace, effectively balances all the warmer colours in the room, while the occasional accessories in creams and whites provide cooler, more refreshing accents against the mellow richness of the overall setting.

four looks to create with yellow

The colour of sunshine and merriment, yellow is always uplifting, but has a mellower side, too. Its natural warmth makes it one of the most welcoming of hues in any room.

Choose it for its light-reflective quality, and then add suitable accessories and accent colours to adapt its mood to suit the style of the room.

△ natural warmth

Let the full range of tones shine through the underlying yellow, and use them to create contrasts and accents within a simple colour scheme. The mellow warmth of this kitchen comes from its rich cream paintwork as well the deeper yellows of the curtains and the crockery. Even the cooking ingredients on the shelves play their part, with jars of amber honey and golden sugar adding their own rich colour.

△ modern opulence

Yellow is such a timeless colour that it can be used to create a sense of opulence in both traditional and contemporary settings. This room uses every means possible to reflect the golden glow of the walls. A huge mirror on the chimneybreast bounces the colour back into the room, and the fireplace is dressed with clusters of gilded accessories, including the rich lustre of gold and copper leaf squares applied along the mantel.

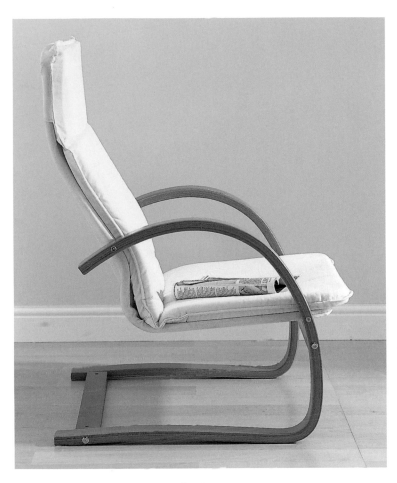

△ streamlined simplicity

The nearly neutral quality of yellow comes into its own here. Although the wall itself is painted in a strong, glowing shade, setting against it the cool, minimal shape of this contemporary chair in restrained, natural tones somehow neutralizes the colour. The drama is removed from the yellow shade so that it blends with the pale wood of the floorboards and provides a mellow background instead of a bold contrast.

△ morning gold

A real rise-and-shine colour, yellow is wonderful to wake up to. It is active and stimulating to kick-start the day, and cheerful at all other times. This bedroom scheme combines the richest golds tinged with touches of deeper rust red for bedcovers and scatter cushions, with softer creams for the bedside table and lampbase, and highlights of pure white linen to add extra accent.

four shades of yellow to try

1

2

3

4

gold

This is the colour to wake you up and keep you alert. It is a rich, glowing shade that will reflect morning light and give an effect of bright sunshine all day long, so it is especially good for illuminating dark or north-facing rooms. It is also a brilliant background for paintings.

- **style:** Glowing, rich, sunny.
- **inspiration:** Sunflowers, egg yolks, Mediterranean sunshine.
- **where to use:** Anywhere you want to warm up a gloomy space. This colour will fill the room with sunshine all year round.
- **watch points:** If you use it in a bedroom, you need to be able to cope with its strong wake-up character. This is not a shade to promote rest or tranquillity.
- **mix with:** Mediterranean blues and greens, hot pinks and strong violets.

1

lemon

An invigorating shade with a very intense colour, this yellow seems to radiate light. Its quality is more green than orange, so it works well with natural greens and stone colours.

- **style:** Sharp, fresh, fizzy.
- **inspiration:** Citrus fruits, sherbet, sorbets.
- **where to use:** Kitchens – to keep the mood fresh and active. Bathrooms – to recharge your batteries. This is a thoroughly energizing colour.
- **watch points:** Be careful in bedrooms and living rooms, where lemon may be too acidic, and in hallways, where it could create a harsh first impression of the house.
- **mix with:** Pinks and violets to increase the energy. Muted stone to tone it down. Cornflower blue to balance the warmth.

butter

This deeper yellow provides a warmer effect. It is not so much of a space-maker, but is welcoming and enclosing – perfect for rooms where you want to feel relaxed or which will be used for entertaining.

- **style:** Natural, warm, comfortable.
- **inspiration:** Sand, honey, hayfields.
- **where to use:** Most living areas – this is a comfortable shade with a good everyday feel plus plenty of warmth to brighten up evening rooms.
- **watch points:** All that warmth and sunshine can feel a bit rich in a room that gets a lot of natural light.
- **mix with:** White, cream, warm neutrals. Natural wood and wicker.

3

primrose

Soft, pastel shades are the most restful yellows to use, and pale enough to combine well with other colours. Because they are so light, and because they verge on the cooler half of the colour spectrum, they will have a 'receding' effect, making rooms look more spacious.

- **style:** Pale, pretty, adaptable.
- **inspiration:** Primroses, buttermilk, vanilla ice cream.
- **where to use:** Bedrooms, living rooms, country kitchens. As a richer alternative to cream when you want more depth than a pure neutral.
- **watch points:** Not too much to worry about – it is soft enough not to cause problems.
- **mix with:** Pinks, soft blues and turquoises for harmony. Violet and aubergine for contrast. Stronger yellows to bring out its richer accents.

4

mixing yellow with other colours

blue

Blue with yellow always makes an impact, and the bolder the shades, the more dramatic the effect. Shown here is a very confident use of two incredibly rich colours. Set against one another on adjacent walls and hung with a collection of pictures and elaborately framed mirrors, the two colours become part of the background rather than the focus of the furnishings.

green

A natural garden mix, and sitting side by side on the colour wheel, green and yellow look comfortable together. Yellow is cheerful and stimulating, so the calmer, more restful tones of green help to quieten the effect, but the two colours have enough similarity to blend without a harsh contrast. Green alone is not really strong enough to balance yellow, though, so add plenty of whites or neutrals to prevent the yellow from dominating the scheme.

pink

Yellow and pink are a fresh, contemporary mix. Dramatic and zingy, this colour scheme really hots things up, as the two colours are both from the warm end of the colour spectrum. The fuchsia pink used here is very strong, but because yellow is a pure primary, and because it is used consistently over such a large area, it has enough depth of tone to hold its own. It is a brave clash, which works because the amount of pink is carefully limited.

purple

This is not as brave a step as it sounds, because violet, which is mixed from red and blue, is the natural complementary shade to yellow (see page 14) – think of violets and primroses together in spring or of purple pansy heads with their own yellow centres. Here, you can see that the darker cushion creates an opulent, dramatic effect, while the paler lilac suggests a softer, more romantic look.

red

Full-strength reds and yellows can fight horribly and be hard work to live with, so it is safer to opt for softer pinks (see opposite, bottom) or a colourwashed terracotta like the background used here. Combine it with a sunny, golden yellow so that the two shades work harmoniously and echo each other's warm, glowing accents.

neutrals

Most yellows work best when highlighted with fresh whites, but this interesting alternative creates a subtler look. The strongest yellow is actually the gold of the floorboards, while the walls are painted a more muted shade of sand, with the oatmeal sofa fabric adding a genuinely 'neutral' element to the colour scheme. It is restrained but warm – a good combination for a cold or gloomy room.

sources of inspiration

Yellow has a knack of making rooms – and people – feel instantly better, so trust your instincts and pick up on interesting shades wherever you come across them. Natural settings will provide masses of ideas – from sunshine and sandy beaches to cornfields and autumn leaves – but you will also find inspiration in manmade colour and modern accessories. Pick out the yellow spines in a bookcase, or the yellow jumpers stacked in a shop display. Remember that this is a children's colour, full of life and energy, so indulge in the sherbetty shades of the local sweetshop and take a look at the brightly painted toys and plastic gadgets lined up on your children's playroom shelves.

△ children's parties

See how wonderfully glowing jellies and sugar icing mix together on a brightly spread table. Edible yellows have a refreshing, zesty style that other colours just cannot match.

▷ bright berries

Look for unusual golds and creams lurking among the more familiar red berries. These glossy, gleaming surfaces bring out the rich, luxurious quality of yellow.

△ fabric shops

Look for the freshest shades and the crispest cottons to bring a spring living room to life. Gingham checks, candy stripes, polka dots and floral sprigs all suit yellow's bright, cheerful character.

△ spring flowers

Be inspired by yellow buds, shoots and petals, as well as the pollen-rich centres of flowers in other shades. Yellow is the most joyful colour, full of optimism and rejuvenation, so use it to flood the house with sunshine.

▷ domestic finds

Sometimes a single item can spark off a whole colour scheme, so look out for bright gadgets and appliances that appeal to you. Don't assume that functional equipment needs to be a functional colour – splash out on more imaginative shades and make them part of the furnishings.

green

Fresh and **rejuvenating**, green is the colour of **wellbeing**, fertility, spring foliage and summer **meadows**. Learn to love its calming nature and use it to breathe **new life** into tired rooms.

why green works

For many years the colour green was perceived as the poor relation in decorating terms. It was considered not as fresh as blue or as pretty as pink, and was associated more with the outdoor world than with interior design. But the myths have now been dispelled, and shades of green are recognized as among the most restful and tranquil of furnishing colours. Challenging all those misconceptions with enormous versatility, it can be soft and pretty, bold and zesty, deep and leafy, or take on a host of subtle silvery shades reminiscent of moss and lichen. Enjoy playing with the potential green offerings, and have fun picking accessories from this interesting colour group. Just be careful when choosing paints – always try them out in a good-sized sample area first as green paint colours can be deceptive in small quantities and different lights.

△ versatility

A relative newcomer to the contemporary decorating palette, green has worked hard to overcome its uncertain image by turning itself into one of the most versatile colours around. As a result, you are just as likely to find it in classic paint shades and decorative wallpapers as in country-style gingham or plaid fabrics and bold modern or abstract prints. Often, the shift in character is achieved by something as simple as a change in shade or the addition of a particular trimming or detail. Texture plays a part, too. Green is a colour that adapts well to variation in texture, so that it can be sleek and luxurious in rich velvet, fresh and practical in chunky chequered wool, or subtle and durable in hardwearing drill. This adaptable quality makes green remarkably easy to live with, so experiment with different shades and patterns to find the mix that suits your setting.

▽ calm

Green has a calmness unlike any other colour, and is a natural peacemaker. If you think of it in its outdoor setting of garden or countryside, it always manages to work in harmony with dozens of different flower and leaf colours, despite its own variations in shade and tone. Artists, for example, will point out that the colour of grass has a surprising amount of blue in it, and that leaves can never be represented by a 'standard' green. This sense of natural balance can make green a wonderfully relaxing background for bedrooms and living rooms, where it provides a soothing, meditative setting. To maintain the feeling of calm, don't add any sharp accent colours, but instead keep to mellow, toning shades that blend into one another, especially creams and neutrals, which reflect the natural quality of the underlying green.

△ freshness

Green brings the garden indoors, filling rooms with a sense of the open air and giving interior spaces something of the style of a conservatory or orangery. Pick the right shades, and green can throw off its calming, soothing character to become vital and invigorating, bursting with suggestions of growth and regeneration, or glowing with Caribbean carnival festivity. Think of the fruity, zesty shades of lime and apple, or the beauty of a summer lawn sparkling in the dew. You will find freshness in different types of green – the yellower shades are exuberant and stimulating, while those with more blue in them are cool and watery. The freshest greens are wonderful for enlivening working areas such as kitchens, as well as creating a crisp, refreshing mood in bathrooms and daytime living rooms – try them out in rooms that don't get much sun and see how much lighter the areas become.

◁ **This translucent mint green is cool and restful and creates an elegant, faintly oriental background for decorative plates and simple flowers.**

▷ **The slightly darker floral motif adds depth and accent to the pale green, but isn't obtrusive enough to appear as a definite pattern.**

the green living room

This crisp, slightly translucent shade of green is both restful and distinctive, making it an excellent living room colour. The living room tends to be in use at all times of the day, so the shade you choose for it needs to be able to adapt to different purposes and varying amounts of light, without losing its essential character or tone. The green used here has an almost oriental glow to it. Pale but rich, cool but luminous, it is a beautifully liquid shade with a remarkable purity of tone that provides a good background for furnishings and accessories in other greens and in contrasting colours from the pastel spectrum.

decorative display

Green is a particularly good shade to use as a background for display items – paintings and photographs are thrown into sharp relief by its strong character. If you are worried about choosing colours to set against it, you can opt for the fail-safe option of sticking to a monochrome display. A collection of black and white photos carefully arranged against this vivid green will turn the room into an instant art gallery. For a more classical look, you could use copies of traditional black and white engravings to recreate the print-room effect that was popular in the 18th century. This involves pasting photocopies of images directly on to a rich-coloured wall in a formal arrangement and then 'linking' them with decorative

papers. Specialist decorating shops still sell ornamental papers designed to look like silk cord, bows, rosettes and tassels, so that you can create your own authentic print-room setting.

Don't be frightened of introducing more colour to offset the green. You need not use strong contrasts or large areas – take inspiration from the garden, and look for flower shades that sit happily among green foliage. Soft pinks and lilacs are among the easiest colours to work with, as in the decorative paintwork of the plate display shown here. Using real flowers – the tulips in the hearth and roses on the mantelpiece – as a natural palette, the china picks out a range of floral colours and then mixes them with leafy greens that contrast gently with the cooler, bluer green of the background wall.

natural accessories

This calm, restful green sets a mood of easy elegance, so the key to adding furnishings is to keep them simple and not clutter the room with too much stuff. The natural wood floor used here is neat and understated, and the neutral-coloured furnishings are enlivened with a touch of soft colour and plenty of varied textures – woollen blankets and loose-woven linen chair covers contrast with the smooth stone of the fireplace and the curved back of the little decorative chair.

the green bedroom

A single shade of green can be deepened and softened into many contrasting tones, creating masses of variety within a very limited palette. It is the simplicity of colour that gives this traditional-style bedroom its natural, tranquil air. Starting with a pale apple green – a garden shade that is perfect for country-effect furnishings – the scheme is built up layer by layer with accents suggesting gentle mossy shades and deeper leaf tones. The whole effect is soft and restful at night, fresh and light reflective in the morning – an irresistible setting for a romantic bedroom complete with all the trimmings.

gentle contrasts

There is an old-fashioned quality to this colour scheme that provides just the right background for traditional furnishings such as the four-poster bed. The bed itself is an opportunity to add swathes of extra fabric, which contribute their own element to the colour scheme. Bedlinens, pillows and covers can be layered one on top of another to introduce subtle contrasts – gingham checks and embroidered details adding depth to the plain background. Soft drapes in voile or muslin help to filter the light, while adding to the sense of romance. Hung around the bed, these panels will pick up the pale glow of the walls and let some of the colour show through the translucent weave, so that the pure white blends with the green

background rather than standing out starkly against it. For the same reason, the frame of the bed has been painted in a soft matt colourwash that lets the grain of the wood show through rather than hiding it behind a bright white finish.

texture and accent

Look closely and you will also see how a clever colour scheme and well-chosen furnishings can completely alter a room's underlying structure and architecture. The modern window betrays that this is a contemporary building, yet the colours and accessories create a far more established effect, and a cottagey, country atmosphere. A slim, painted, carved screen conceals the functional heating panel, and one corner of the room is fitted with painted, decorative shelves to hold pretty ceramics. The mixed textures of the fabrics and other surfaces increase the sense of country comfort. The crisp linens, sheer muslin and heavily patterned window curtains all provide variety, while details such as natural, woven storage baskets and the chenille bobble trimming add contrasting depth of interest. To continue the effect, you could incorporate simple cream calico – the rough, slubby surface is a perfect foil for the floaty sheers. Pretty broderie anglaise with its delicately cut patterns would add character, while for a touch of accent colour you could introduce the occasional accessory in a pink sprigged floral.

four looks to create with green

Light green has a quiet, adaptable character that mixes comfortably with natural wood and flower shades, but also suits cooler, more minimal furnishing schemes. Combine it with pretty pastels for an old-fashioned country setting, or with sleek, streamlined chrome and glass to create a practical, contemporary look.

△ old-fashioned romance

Use fresh green as a background for traditional fabrics such as checked linen, fine lace, floral chintz and crisp white cotton. This look is perfect for bedrooms and living rooms. Decorate the walls with a wreath of dried roses, or with an understated collection of delicate flower prints or faded watercolours. Set a tray with traditional linens and pretty china, and add a spray of fresh flowers as a final scented flourish.

△ sleek modernism

Combine cool green wallpaper with laminated wood and sleek chrome for a clean, contemporary look. Great for studies, offices, kitchens and hallways, this mix has a practical, functional feel that focuses and refreshes the mind. Look for streamlined furniture with no unnecessary decoration, then accessorize with details such as pale wood bookshelves, stainless steel lampbases and filing boxes that emphasize the smart, unobtrusive lines and contrast with the more traditional feel of the patterned paper.

△ country charm

Take your cue from the natural quality of the shade and use it as the starting point for a rustic collection of potted plants and simple spongeware china. Painted in matt green against an old-rose wallpaper, this country-style shelf unit provides a gentle background for warm, autumnal earth colours including old leather books and weathered terracotta containers, as well as the natural green of cacti and wild flowers.

△ classic elegance

Pale green works beautifully with soft neutral shades to create sunny, light-filled colour schemes. Keep to the prettiest creams and whites for upholstery fabrics, flooring and accessories, with bleached or white-painted wood so that the restful effect is not interrupted by blocks of dark furniture. Touches of complementary soft reds and pinks (see pages 112–113) will provide a little more colour if you want to add accent or definition.

four shades of green to try

moss

This is an old-fashioned shade, but with lots of natural tone making it comfortable to live with. It is not for rooms where you want to feel lively and invigorated, but provides a restful background for traditional furniture.

- **style:** Sober, traditional, quiet.
- **inspiration:** Woodland, shady gardens, asparagus soup.
- **where to use:** Formal dining rooms and book-lined studies. Traditional living rooms complete with gilt-framed pictures and china cabinets.
- **watch points:** Dark green can have a deadening effect, so add plenty of fresh, subtle highlights with cream or very pale pink.
- **mix with:** Cream, old leather, dark wood furniture and flooring.

1

apple

If you think of green as a natural country colour, this is one of the most countrified shades. Soft and pretty, it is a good light reflector, and will adapt easily to both modern and traditional furnishings.

- **style:** Pure, fresh, calming.
- **inspiration:** Granny Smith apples, willow fronds, creamy heads of *Alchemilla mollis* (lady's mantle).
- **where to use:** Almost anywhere. This shade – especially if layered in a colourwashed effect like the bathroom here – is incredibly restful and versatile. Try it in country-style bedrooms, bathrooms and living rooms.
- **watch points:** Be careful the room doesn't become too yellow – add contrasting accents if necessary.
- **mix with:** Autumnal reds, russets and deeper greens, or clear summery pastels.

2

jade

This cool, elegant green, with its hint of aqua, is fresh and modern, a summer shade with a distinctive character and a style of its own.

- **style:** Cool, refreshing, faintly oriental.
- **inspiration:** Mountain streams, peppermint.
- **where to use:** Bedrooms – try it with a futon-style bed and a decorative folding screen. Bathrooms, to make the most of its translucent, watery quality. Living rooms, especially a room that opens on to the garden.
- **watch points:** Don't add strong colours – they will smother this gentle shade.
- **mix with:** White, pale woods such as bamboo, delicate black lacquer.

3

grass

A mid-tone green with a lot of strength, this shade is poised between classic and contemporary. It has a dense quality similar to some of the traditional 19th-century paint colours, but a slightly lighter finish which makes it more adaptable.

- **style:** Strong, clean, stimulating.
- **inspiration:** Spring leaves, summer lawns.
- **where to use:** Kitchens – mix it with cream for a classic pantry look. Well-lit or south-facing living rooms.
- **watch points:** Try sample paint colours over a good-sized area before committing yourself as it is difficult to gauge the effect from a small patch.
- **mix with:** Cream, blue, pinks, purples – most flower colours will work as this is their natural background shade in the garden.

4

mixing green with other colours

red

These yellowy greens have no real impact until a splash of complementary red (see page 14) is introduced to bring them to life. It doesn't take much. A single red cushion among the others offsets their much quieter, retiring tones, adding accent and definition to the sofa in the same way that punctuation marks make sense of a sentence and give it a structure.

neutrals

Greens and neutrals are among the most natural of colour pairings. Here, a mixture of stone and cream shades are used to create a balance of warm and cool tones – the greyish tinge in the ceramics echoes the cool aqua green of the upholstery, while the cream of the cushions and lamp adds a warmer touch.

purple

This is a beautifully restful combination of two secondary colours together (green mixed from blue and yellow, and purple from red and blue) so that you get a muted effect, much subtler than the clash of two primaries. It is reminiscent of flower shades, too. Think of lilac or lavender against a backdrop of green leaves and you can see why green and purple work together so naturally.

blue

By varying the shades of both blue and green elements, this kitchen creates a fresh, country-style scheme in which neither colour dominates but both play an important part. On the blue team, there is dark navy, bright cobalt and a lighter, turquoise shade, while the greens are represented by bright leaf colours and a more muted, olive tone for the coffee pot and rug. The result is a comfortable balance with no jarring contrasts.

pink

The frothy heads of these pale green guelder-roses are offset to perfection by the addition of a few blooms of deep pink ranunculus. Because the pink is a diluted shade of red, the natural complementary colour to green (see page 14), the two colours intensify each other, but without clashing as stridently as full strength red and green might do.

yellow

The green of this kitchen is already so zesty and fresh that adding yellow simply brings out its lighter tones. The fabric of the simple curtain at the window incorporates the yellow quite clearly – it looks as though one shade has been 'dragged' over the other to create a streaky paint effect. Following this lead, the two colours have been blended in a chequerboard painted tile design that links the yellow units with the green walls.

sources of inspiration

The world is full of inspiration for shades of green.

Countryside, woodland, parks and gardens are packed with so many natural greens that you can hardly take them all in. Layers of leaves, ferns, stalks and grass all add their own colour, and because each one is natural, they never seem to clash, however dramatic the mix. Enjoy the colour saturation for its own pleasure, and then learn to distinguish the different shades from one another, for example pale silver sage, bright grass, dark pine needles, and plan where you can use them. Select greens from your fruit bowl, too, and from the vegetable rack – dark blue-green cabbage leaves, crisp shiny watercress, zingy bright limes and pale glowing grapes.

△ garden leaves

Trees and plants provide a vast range of natural greens from which to choose a shade. Enjoy the different colours and textures to be found in a single border, from pale silver to dark forest green.

◁ herbs and salads

Think of the mixes that work best in a herb garden or salad bowl and look for shades to match them. Basil leaves, sprays of rosemary, young spinach and fresh rocket will all provide inspiration.

△ fresh fruit
Crisp and zesty, fruit provides decorating colour that is good enough to eat. Grapes, gooseberries, greengages and apples are full of fresh inspiration.

△ sweetshop selection
Sweetshops are a mine of inspiration because of all those bright wrappers lined up next to one another. Pick up on the textures, too, from filmy tissue to gleaming metallic foil.

◁ blossom and blooms
You don't expect to find green petals, but sometimes the colour of the stem bleeds into the flower head itself – a wonderfully subtle effect in white or cream blooms.

neutrals

The classic sophistication of **coffee** and **cream**, the natural elegance of **stone** and **charcoal** – neutral shades always make up in **subtlety** for what they lack in colour.

why neutrals work

Don't be fooled by the name – colours are never completely neutral. Grey and brown may not be so pure as the primaries, or so easy to define as the rest of the colour spectrum, but they still have their own personalities and are capable of creating very different effects. From the cool shades of chalk white, slate grey and deep graphite to the warm tones of buttercream, honey and rich chocolate, this is an intriguing palette with masses of variety.

Neutral colours are not necessarily the safe option they are always assumed to be – you cannot just ask for 'cream' and assume it will suit any space and any purpose – but it is wonderfully subtle and adaptable. Think about the direction the room faces, the amount of light it gets and the mood you want to establish before deciding whether you need the colour to be cool or warm, pale or deep.

△ comfort

Paint a room in a neutral colour and you have a background that will adapt to any style or age. Such a wonderfully versatile setting lets you switch your furnishings from cool and minimal to rich and textured, according to your mood and changing fashions. Instead of having to repaint and totally refurnish each time a new look comes into vogue, you can just make simple adjustments while maintaining your own style. Keep the look clean and uncluttered or add traditional warmth and texture – the understated colour will adapt to both. Best of all, the overall effect is one of comfort and relaxation because it relies on feel as much as appearance. Neutral furnishings are about easy living rather than making an impression, so all that really matters is that you feel good in the room you have created.

▽ simplicity

However sophisticated some of the effects may be, there is a basic, practical character underlying neutral furnishings. This is the colour of wood, basketware, leather and rush matting – simple, robust materials concerned more with function than appearance. The bonus is that they look good, too, so that 'simple' style has acquired its own status in decorating terms. Trustworthy and unassuming, creams, whites, greys and browns work effortlessly together without any need for careful colour scheming, and their natural surfaces provide plenty of instant texture and contrast. Soft white towels, woven and plaited baskets, dappled stone and slate, the planks and slats of wooden furniture all combine to create a plain, serviceable look. The greater the amount of texture, the more rustic the effect tends to be, so this is the route to go if you want country-style simplicity.

△ blank canvas

Strip out the colour that usually gives a room its immediate impact, and you are forced to look at it more closely and find more imaginative ways to bring it to life. Without the distraction of colour, you get back to the essence of the room's shape and character, leaving you with a blank canvas to play with. It sounds like a daunting prospect, but professional designers often recommend painting a room off white as a starting point for a new decorating scheme. From here you can build up shades and tones, and introduce stronger colour if you want to. It is also a chance to try out different effects using line and texture. As an exercise, forget about creating a complete room and experiment instead with varying shapes and shadows to see how they work together.

◁ **Calm and contemporary, this subtle mixture of creams and browns demonstrates the versatility of the neutral palette, from pale honey gold to rich chocolate brown.**

▷ **Natural materials like basketweave and woodgrain provide extra interest, and echo the textured effect of this subtly stippled wallpaper pattern.**

the neutral living room

This combination of coffee-and-cream colours creates a room you could move straight into – effortlessly comfortable but defined by an understated sense of style. The overall impression is sleek and contemporary, but there is a surprising amount of richness in the texture. The clean lines give it a classic feel, which makes it a good setting for traditional furniture designs as well as modern pieces. The tone is established by the coffee-coloured walls, a wonderfully warm background which, despite its neutral shade, provides a lot of depth because of its gently textured pattern. From a distance, this doesn't register at all, but up close you realize it looks like a miniature animal print, giving the surface a mottled effect. So it is a classic colour with a modern touch, and the perfect partner for the wooden floor, which mixes pale boards in subtly variegated tones to create dappled areas of light and shade.

variety of tone

The neutral room challenges our notion of 'neutrality' by incorporating so many colours and contrasts within its limited palette. Try giving each element its own specific colour instead of categorizing them all as cream or brown, and you realize the huge variety of shades involved. There is the honey-coloured wicker of the side tables and storage baskets; the rich caramel of the tall wooden cabinet and the picture frame; the cushions, ranging

from soft vanilla through natural oatmeal to jet black; and the cool slate grey that has been picked out from the patterned rug and echoed in vases on the hearth and mantelpiece. Most dramatic of all, there is the glorious rich chestnut of the sofa, a rich, chocolaty shade with a surface soft enough to provide extra warmth but with a sheen that catches the light and creates interesting accents.

line and texture

There is something other than colour at work here, conveying the way in which a room's style can be defined just as strongly by line and texture. Without the instant impact of colour to distract you, these have to work much harder to provide areas of focus and contrast to keep you interested. The dramatic fireplace plays a key role in this, strong and angular as it is against all the soft upholstery and creating moody grey shadows with each of its recessed sections. The skirting, painted white to contrast with the coffee-coloured walls, is traced by a paper border just above it to highlight the room's classic proportions and give it more definition. And throughout the room, the contrasting textures – soft rug, smooth leather and plaited wicker – add depth and character.

warm neutrals

△ ivory white

This is a rich, creamy shade that dispels any hint of chill. There is just enough yellow in it to warm up the room without adding actual colour, so it is perfect for a north-facing room, especially a small one where you want to open up the space. It is completely natural, and creates a wonderfully restful background against which to layer other creams and whites, with curtains, candles, chair covers and tablelinens all adding their own accents.

△ honey

The golden warmth of this wood tone is highlighted by the blocks of cooler grey painted on it. Even the seat cover, which is creamy rather than brilliant white, looks cool by comparison. Wood is an excellent way of adding warm neutrals, and this honey shade is easy to supply with laminate flooring, old pine furniture and a host of details from curtain poles to picture frames.

△ coffee

Subtle and understated, this is a classic shade with impeccable contemporary credentials. It doesn't disappear into the background – on the contrary it has enough depth of tone to provide a major element in your furnishing scheme – but it has a gift for mixing effortlessly with both neutrals and other colours. To get the best from it, try it out in different fabric textures such as linen, suede and corduroy.

△ chocolate

Dark browns can be oppressive, but there is a clean quality about this purplish shade. Rich and warm, without becoming hot or treacly, it has a natural elegance that translates equally well into classic polished wood furniture and modern chunky corduroy sofa coverings. Use it in small quantities to add rich contrasts to softer creams and create areas of depth and drama.

cool neutrals

△ bright white

This is the purest of all neutrals – a completely blank canvas waiting for you to put your mark on it. There is no obvious hint of any other colour in its stark tone, so it is up to you to define its character by adding appropriate furnishings and accessories. It can be too cold, particularly in north-facing rooms that don't get much natural light, but if you have a sun-filled room with large windows, this is the way to keep it cool.

△ grey stone

As greys go, this soft shade with its silvery accents is not one of the coldest, but it is still cool enough to make most whites look positively warm by comparison, as you can see from the milky tones of these jugs. It is a very elegant colour, neat and contained, which mixes well with whites and creams to give a calm, delicate effect. You may find it slightly deadening as a wall colour, but it is excellent for furnishings and details.

△ slate grey

This is where grey almost meets blue, as the neutral shade is shot through with inky colour. Slate itself, a classic material for conservatory floors and kitchen worktops, has a layered, textured finish that gives it plenty of variety, and it is a good idea to recreate this effect where you use the colour. Look for chalky Mediterranean-style paints with a powdery finish, and add plenty of textured fabrics so that you get silver highlights among the grey shadows.

△ graphite

A deep grey with a moody character, graphite has a natural affinity with cool, modern settings and streamlined furnishings. Often paired with sharp black accents and sleek steel or chrome fittings, it usually has a strong and slightly masculine style. However, it can take on a prettier feel if you combine it with soft lilacs and silvers, and include more decorative furniture shapes.

adding texture

If you are sticking to a neutral palette, without stronger colours to add accent and contrast, texture becomes all important in defining the room's character. Fabric finishes, wall surfaces, flooring and furniture all add distinctive texture, taking the place of colour very effectively.

△ textured fabrics

Use fabrics with plenty of texture to show that you can create pattern without obvious colour. Combining contrasting weaves will give a greater sense of depth – slubby linens, velvety suedes, luxurious furs and thick-furrowed cord all add their own style and feel, and knitted throws can be layered over the top. Use details such as buttons and piping to give the mixed fabrics a neat, tailored finish so that they don't look too random.

△ natural weaves

Natural floorcoverings such as coir, sisal, jute and seagrass create a subtle, muted background for furniture and fabrics. Even the plain weaves have masses of texture, but for more defined pattern look for herringbone or chequered designs. Continue the natural theme by adding practical baskets for storage and filing. These useful containers are brilliant for storage in bedrooms and bathrooms.

▽ paint finishes

Even plain, neutral walls can provide an element of pattern. Paintwork creates a variety of textured effects, especially if you combine different finishes – matt, eggshell and gloss – so that they reflect and absorb different levels of light. Here, the patchy colour on the little table adds a distressed, antique effect, as though the cream paintwork has gradually worn away to let the darker undercoat show through, while the wall is painted with a thick, chalky finish so that it has the texture of rough plaster.

△ relief pattern

More definite pattern can be provided by applying decorative details, still within the neutral palette. Plasterwork, moulding and wooden panelling all create elegant lines when painted to blend with the wall or to contrast in a subtly different shade. Make a display of china, too, layering whites and creams against one another to create relief patterns in a neutral colour.

sources of inspiration

Because of their subtle, unobtrusive nature, neutral colours won't attract your attention as conspicuously as the more decided shades. It is easy for creams, greys and soft whites to pass you by when stronger colours are shouting to be noticed. But once you start looking, you will find invaluable inspiration and become aware of contrasts and differences you never realized existed. Browse through a good stationery shop and see how many different whites and creams are available for you to write on. Check your garden shed for varied tones of wood, string, stone and sacking. And indulge in the rich shades of a fresh coffee store, with glossy beans ranging in colour from burnt caramel to dark mahogany.

△ stones and pebbles

The mottled, streaked surfaces of stones and pebbles provide their own miniature palettes of neutral shades, all blending into one another with natural harmony and contrast. You'll find both cool greys and warm creams, as well as darker, moody tones.

◁ larder supplies

Raid your kitchen cupboards and refrigerator for a stock of inspiring shades. Honey, nuts, brown sugar, cream and butter all suggest rich, intriguing colours to translate into furnishings.

△ seaside finds

Beachcombing trips will uncover shells, driftwood and other seaside finds such as dried starfish, all of which provide their own layers of whites, creams and greys.

△ fabric swatches

Trawl through fabric departments for materials with plenty of textural interest. Chunky woollens, soft velvets, loose-woven linens and tightly-matted felts will provide distinctive contrasts.

◁ rural treasures

Take a lead from countryside treasures and farmyard finds – feathers, eggs and natural straw shades are mellow and unpretentious and provide a surprising amount of variety.

quick colour

Adapt and **experiment**. Take the fast track to colour by introducing new **accents** and trying out different **accessories**. Paint, fabric, ceramics and flowers will **transform** any space.

paint

Paint is one of the easiest and most enjoyable ways to add colour quickly and effectively. You don't need to repaint an entire room in order to transform its colour scheme or change its atmosphere. The beauty of paint is how fast its effects can be seen, so adding a few accent colours to offset the existing shades is the best route to an instant new look.

△ simple stripes

Painted stripes add instant colour to a plain white wall, and take far less effort than all-over colour. Broad vertical stripes can mimic the effect of a wallpaper and will help to heighten a low ceiling. Horizontal stripes are more unusual and will make a small room or narrow area seem wider. Decide on the position of your stripes, using a spirit level to check the horizontals, and mark out guidelines in pencil before painting on your colour. For a neat, sharp line, mask the outer edges of each stripe with masking tape; for a softer, freehand effect, just paint up to the pencil line by eye.

△ border lines

Windows, woodwork and other architectural features can be highlighted by borders of colour to contrast with the main background. Here, a border of deep pink outlines the window and continues along the wall to make an improvised dado rail against the bold orange background. Again, you need a spirit level to check that the horizontal lines are straight, and masking tape to give your stripes a clean edge. To add an extra element of pattern, you can then decorate the border with a stamped motif – in this room the simple coil shape has been stamped in the original wall colour to unify the whole effect.

△ chequerboard floor

Painted floors are wonderfully simple, much cheaper than carpet and give you the option of changing the design as often as you want. It may take a weekend to complete the necessary number of coats – but the advantage is that you can do it yourself rather than having to wait for new flooring to be professionally laid. Look for specialist floor paint, which is extra hardwearing, or use several coats of emulsion and finish with a clear matt varnish to protect the surface. Chequerboards are one of the most satisfying patterns to try. Clean the floorboards thoroughly and deal with any loose nails, then paint the whole area with the lighter of your two paint colours – you will probably need more than one coat. When the paint is completely dry, mark out your chequerboard, then mask off alternate squares and paint these in the darker colour.

△ harlequin drawers

Shabby furniture or cheap modern designs can acquire an individual designer look if you transform them with fresh colour. Choose your colour to suit the style of the room. Use pale, light-reflective shades for a spacious, elegant setting, muted earthy tones for a practical, understated effect reminiscent of the American Shaker style, or bright, cheerful hues for a country-cottage look. Here, alternate drawers have been painted in contrasting blues and lilacs for a child's room. Coat the furniture with a wood primer first, then add your top coat. Oil-based eggshell paint creates the best effect, combining a natural matt finish with a tough, washable surface – but for an even quicker colour, you can use water-based emulsion paint and seal it with a coat of wax.

fabrics

Fabrics are one of the most 'portable' of decorating elements, adding colour in varying quantities of plain shades and decorative pattern. Cushions, curtains, tablecloths and furniture covers can all be used to introduce contrasting shades or balance an existing scheme. Use the texture of the fabric to emphasize the character of the colours, picking crisp cool cottons for watery blues and greens, and rich velvet or wool for warm pinks and golds.

△ peg rail curtain

There is no need for elaborate frills and flounces – a simple curtain in a colour that suits the room is just as effective. Here, a panel of woven red plaid has been edged with a border of grass green to match the colour of the tablecloth and lamp, and then trimmed with a row of fabric loops to make an incredibly quick and easy heading. These loops simply slot on to the pegs of a wooden rail.

◁ cupboard fronts

Kitchen shelves can be fronted with fabric if you are short of time or money to fit proper base units. It is also a good option if the space is too narrow for cupboard doors to open comfortably. Fit the front of the worktop with a slim rail – the kind normally sold for hanging utensils – then cut lengths of fabric to fit the drop from the rail to the floor. Punch a row of metal eyelet holes along the top of the fabric panels, then thread them on to the rail like curtains.

▽ contrasting cushions

Cushions add splashes of instant colour to chairs, sofas and beds. Small and inexpensive, cushions are the most casual and relaxed accessories, easy to work into your scheme and quick to change when you want a new look – not for nothing are they known as scatter cushions. Whatever the background colour, cushions can add accent and contrast, either to match other furnishings in the room, or to introduce a new element to the scheme. Here, for instance, a mixture of mid- and dark blues in simple checks and stripes provides the only colour in an otherwise neutral room, making the sofa a focus of interest as well as a place of comfort.

△ covers and trimmings

Upholstery is a key part of a room's furnishings, and can provide an essential element of colour. Just introducing a single chair in a bright fabric will enliven plain wood and pale walls. Here, the chair fabric has also been used to cover the notebook on the desktop and creates a basic colour palette to which other fabrics can be matched. The little stationery bag is made from a different floral pattern, but in the same colours, and is tied with a strip of the original fabric to create a contrasting trim.

Slip-over chair covers provide the chance to change your colour scheme even more quickly. If you tend to tire of furnishings fairly regularly, look for designs such as director's chairs, whose fabric 'slings' can be removed and replaced, and buy chairs and sofas with loose covers rather than fixed upholstery.

ceramics

From hand-crafted pottery and recycled glass to delicate porcelain and crystal, ceramics come in a wonderful array of shades, ready to be displayed on table tops and in china cabinets. Use them to add accent colour around the house and don't throw out broken china or chipped tiles – the pieces can always be used to make mosaic effects.

△ coloured glass

Glass can be as colourful as china, but the key to displaying it effectively is to position it where the light can shine through it. Windowsills, glass shelves and light fittings are perfect places for glass. Think how beautiful coloured droplets look in chandeliers and clustered around candlesticks – glowing and iridescent, the glass acquires jewel-like brilliance and casts tinted reflections on to surrounding surfaces. Make the most of coloured glass when setting a table or serving drinks, and you can use it as part of your colour scheme, choosing shades to match flowers or fabrics, or to contrast with your china.

△ tile style

Ceramic tiles are an integral part of the colour scheme in kitchens and bathrooms and one of the decisions you make when choosing fittings and paint shades. But you don't need a whole wall of them to make an impact. A few coloured tiles set into a run of white is enough to brighten the room. Similarly, a tiled splashback behind a sink or washbasin will provide an area of contained colour that works brilliantly in a plain white room. If there is no existing colour scheme with which your tiles have to match or coordinate, you can be as bold as you like in choosing rainbow shades that create their own miniature palette.

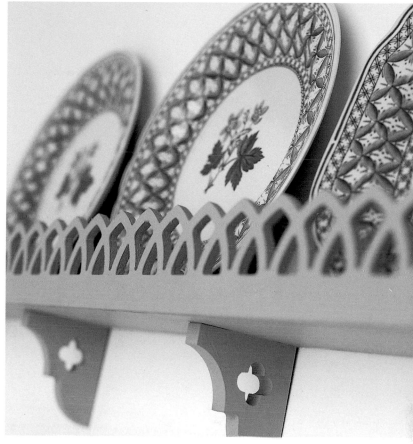

△ dresser displays

One of the best ways to show off your china is on a traditional dresser, which offers the chance to mix different colours and patterns, and to change the arrangement as often as you want. The great thing about dressers is that by providing functional storage for the tableware they hold, they somehow make a unified display of any number of pieces. One of the best combinations is the random blue and white mix typical of classic country kitchens, in which different patterns are unified by a toning colour scheme. Here, a collection of chunky, hand-painted ceramics is given the same treatment, with soft pink providing a link between the contrasting spotted and flowered patterns, and a few bright red tumblers taking the spotted theme one bold step further.

△ shelf life

Plates add beautiful colour and should not be restricted to the dining table. Line them up on a rack or display shelf, or hang them on the wall itself. A plate rack running around the top of the wall at picture rail height provides perfect display space for a set of matching plates or jugs. Similar shelves can be added – either by panelling the lower part of the wall and topping it with a plinth, or by fixing individual decorative shelves, such as the one shown here. This one works particularly well, painted the same blue as the plates themselves and with a crossed-arch design that matches their pattern.

flowers

Fresh flowers inject an instant shot of colour. It is a temporary effect, lasting only as long as the blooms themselves, but that is part of their magic. Each display is unique and precious, yet new looks can be conjured up to replace them once they have gone. The flowers themselves don't need to be exotic or expensive – simple bunches from a market stall will contribute just as much colour and beauty as a formal arrangement.

△ table posies

Cut simple garden flowers to decorate tables and mantelpieces. Here, creamy narcissi and purple grape hyacinths provide fresh spring colour in very informal arrangements. Make use of everyday kitchenware for unusual containers – frosted tumblers, milk jugs and tea pots for short-stemmed flowers, or coffee pots and wine carafes for taller, more elegant displays.

◁ chair decorations

Table settings always provide an opportunity for adding plenty of accent colour, and here is a way to extend the scheme so that it includes the chairs, too. Little bunches of flowers bound with raffia are tied on to the back of each chair to match the table decorations. If you use lilies, as in the picture, be careful to keep the pollen-heavy heads facing outwards so that they don't touch the clothes of the chairs' occupants.

▽ summer garland

The beauty of this effect is that it can be created with artificial flowers as well as fresh, so if you want it to last, look for good-quality silk or paper blooms. A summer version of a traditional Christmas wreath, this garland can be hung on a door or wall or propped on a shelf or mantelpiece. For the base, you need about six or eight thin lengths of natural cane, which can be twisted into a circle and then bound with raffia and ribbon – use coloured raffia for a pretty, summery look. Then push flower stems under the ribbon around the circle. This garland uses cornflowers and rosebuds, but you can vary the blooms to suit the colour scheme of the room.

△ floating blooms

The simplest of all displays makes a wonderful centrepiece for a dining or coffee table, with cut flower heads floating in water so that they form their own patterns – no arranging needed! The blooms need to be densely petalled and wide-spreading to float effectively, so avoid tight buds or soft-petalled flowers such as roses and tulips. Gerberas, marigolds, cornflowers and all kinds of daisy work well – here they are mixed with pale green guelder-roses.

index

acknowledgements

Crown Paints 4, 13 top right, 30 top right, 39 top right, 46 bottom left, 68, 77 left, 78, 78 top right, 88, 94 top right, 94 bottom right, 94 bottom left, 97 bottom, 100, 103 bottom left, 110 top left, 119, 124, 125 right, 127 left, 128 right, 130, 131
Octopus Publishing Group Limited/David Loftus 129 top left
/William Reavell 115 top left
The National Magazine Company Limited 26, 29 right, 36, 38, 39, 44 right, 45 right, 51 top left, 54, 55 bottom left, 80 right, 81 top left, 82 left, 86, 93 left, 108 right, 112 bottom, 113 right, 118, 120, 121, 132 left, 132 right, 134 right, 136 right, 139 left, 139 right
/Greame Ainscough 97 right
/Christian Barnett 35 top left
/Dominic Blackmore 5 top, 23 top, 30, 46 top right, 48 top left, 61 left, 62 top left, 64 bottom, 66 bottom right, 67 top left, 99 top right, 116, 133 right
/Jon Bouchier 67 bottom right
/Clive Bozzard-Hill 82 right
/Paul Bricknell 122 right
/Ginette Chapman 87 bottom left, 126 left
/Polly Eltes 56, 57, 73, 85, 110 bottom left, 123 right, 129 right

/Stewart Grant 12, 65 right, 81 bottom, 84, 94 top left, 122 left
/Jacqui Hurst 103 top right
/Syriol Jones 71 top right, 97 top left
/Derek Lomas 83 right
/David Munns 128 left
/Thomas Odulate 51 bottom left
/Lizzie Orme 7, 8 top, 8 bottom, 9 top, 9 bottom, 20, 23 bottom, 30 bottom left, 34 bottom right, 34 Top Left, 42, 43, 44 left, 46 top left, 49 right, 60 left, 64 right, 65 top left, 70, 81 right, 87 top right, 92 right, 96 right, 110 bottom right, 119 bottom, 123 left, 126 right, 135 left, 136 left
/Ian Parry 28 right, 32 right, 48 right, 71 bottom left, 89, 90, 96 top left
/Debbie Patterson 50 bottom left, 69, 83 bottom left, 98 left, 98 bottom right, 99 bottom right, 101, 114 top right, 114 bottom left, 115 top right
/Colin Poole 48 bottom, 75
/Spike Powell 5 Bottom, 27, 32 top left, 35 top right, 46 bottom right, 76 left, 96 bottom, 117
/Graham Rea 29 left, 40, 41, 49 bottom, 61 right, 62 bottom right
/Trevor Richards 16, 17 top, 17 bottom, 65 bottom, 72, 77 right, 78 top left, 92 left, 109 left, 113 top left, 113 bottom, 133 left, 135 right, 137 left

/Rowland Roques O'Neil 28 left, 51 top right, 53, 58, 59, 62 top right, 62 bottom left, 78 bottom right, 102, 109 right, 134 left, 137 right
/Lucinda Symons 6, 10, 11, 13 bottom left, 14, 15 Top, 15 bottom, 22, 24, 25, 30 top left, 32 bottom left, 33 right, 33 top left, 33 bottom, 35 bottom, 37, 45 left, 50 top right, 52, 55 top right, 60 right, 64 top left, 67 top right, 74, 76 right, 80 top left, 80 bottom, 83 top left, 91, 93 right, 104, 104, 106, 107, 108 left, 110 top right, 112 right, 124 right, 125 left, 127 right, 129 bottom, 138 left, 138 right, 143
/Jon Whittaker 21, 66 top left
/Polly Wreford 99 top left, 112 top left, 115 bottom left
Sandtex Exterior Paints 49 top

Executive editor Anna Southgate
Editor Rachel Lawrence
Senior designer Rozelle Bentheim
Designer Geoff Borin
Picture researcher Christine Junemann
Production controller Louise Hall

the colour wheel

Use the colour wheel overleaf to **experiment** with **harmonizing** or **contrasting** colour schemes. Study the range of effects you can create with different **combinations**.

how to use the colour wheel

This wheel has been designed to explore the colours of the spectrum even further, breaking them down into individual shades to give you as much choice as possible in choosing your decorating colours. To select shades that will work together in a cohesive scheme, turn the wheel until your main decorating colour appears in the window marked 'chosen colour'. The other colours visible through the 'harmonizing' and 'contrasting' windows will make suitable partners, depending on whether you want your scheme to be based on close harmony or the attraction of opposites.